A **BIBLICAL**
POINT OF VIEW ON

ISLAM

KERBY ANDERSON

HARVEST HOUSE PUBLISHERS

EUGENE, OREGON

Cover by Dugan Design Group, Bloomington, Minnesota

Cover Photo © Medioimages / Photodisc / Getty Images

ISLAM
Copyright © 2008 by Kerby Anderson
Published by Harvest House Publishers
Eugene, Oregon 97402
www.harvesthousepublishers.com

Library of Congress Cataloging-in-Publication Data
Anderson, J. Kerby.
Islam / Kerby Anderson.
p. cm.
Includes bibliographical references (p. 121).
ISBN-13: 978-0-7369-2117-6
ISBN-10: 0-7369-2117-6
1. Islam. 2. Islam—Doctrines. 3. Islam—Relations—Christianity. 4. Christianity and other religions—Islam. I. Title.
BP161.3.A64 2008
297—dc22

                                           2007019411

Printed in the United States of America

07 08 09 10 11 12 13 14 15 / VP-SK / 12 11 10 9 8 7 6 5 4 3 2 1

Contents

A Note About Spelling and Translations

How should we spell the various terms associated with Islam? The answer to that question is not easy because writers and scholars use different spellings for many of the same words.

For example, consider the name of Islam's holy book. Different people spell it as Koran, Qur'an, and Al-Quran. And how do you spell the chapters within this book? Again you will find some variations, such as Surah and Sura. How do you spell the name of the founder of Islam? Here are just a few ways you will find his name spelled: Muhammad, Muhammed, Mohammed, and Mahomet.

In general, I have tried to use the spelling that I found most frequently used by others, especially in online dictionaries and encyclopedias. In this volume, Islam's holy book is the Qur'an, and it is divided into 114 Suras. The founder of Islam is Muhammad, who was born into the Quraysh tribe. The major divisions of Islam are Sunni and Shi'a. Their followers are called Sunni Muslims and Shi'ites.

There are numerous translations of the Qur'an done by many scholars. One translation by an English scholar is *The Koran Interpreted: A Translation,* by A.J. Arberry (Touchstone Books, 1996). A well-received translation by a Muslim scholar is *The Holy Qur'an* by Abdullah Yusuf Ali (Tahrite Tarsile Qur'an, Inc., 2001).

INTRODUCTION

WHERE WERE YOU ON SEPTEMBER 11, 2001? Everyone remembers where they were the day America was attacked by terrorists. For days and weeks later, most of us were asking why it happened and what the motivation was for the attacks.

Those of us who speak on issues such as Islam, terrorism, or foreign policy found a ready audience who wanted to know more about what was happening in our world. Was this an isolated incident or will other attacks come? What provoked the events of that day? What do Muslims believe? These are just a few of the questions that surfaced in the weeks following 9/11.

While I was doing various radio programs on that fateful day, I heard hosts and commentators elsewhere quoting from a radio transcript on terrorism that I first recorded 20 years earlier. Another radio transcript on the Probe Ministries Web site, which dealt with Islam and had been recorded ten years earlier, received an enormous number of hits. Clearly, many people were trying to get some perspective on what had happened.

Since 9/11, interest in knowing more about Islam has remained strong. It is one of the more popular topics I give at conferences such as Mind Games and Worldview Weekend. Additional radio programs we have done, such as "Conversations with a Muslim" and "Islam and the Sword," are very popular and have been well received.

Unfortunately, it has become difficult for people to get clear and accurate information about Islam. In the name of political correctness, some have said, "Islam is a religion of peace," and "The God of Islam is the same God as the God of the Jews and the Christians." But such statements are inaccurate, and people deserve to know the truth.

Those who are concerned about Christian missions know that Islam is a major challenge to the spread of the gospel. Just a few decades ago, most of the countries closed to missionaries were Communist countries. Today those closed countries are usually Muslim.

I have written this book to help answer the questions people most frequently ask about Islam. In nine short chapters, we will explore the history and structure of Islam, review some of the misconceptions about Islam and get a biblical perspective, and take some time to put today's conflict in perspective by looking at the Crusades of the past and the clash of civilizations taking place today.

THE HISTORY OF ISLAM

ISLAM IS THE SECOND LARGEST RELIGION in the world, with approximately 1.4 billion adherents. Islam can be found around the globe. The popular notion is that Islam is a religion of the Middle East, but there are actually more Muslims in Asia (60 percent) than in the Arab world (22 percent) and sub-Saharan Africa (12 percent). The country with the most Muslims today is not an Arab country, but Indonesia, which is in Southeast Asia.

A strategic geographical area for Christian missionary efforts today is known as the "10/40 window." It is so named because the region lies between 10 degrees latitude and 40 degrees latitude north. If you look at a map, you will see this region is dominated by Islamic nations.

Islam is a monotheistic religion based upon the holy book known as the Qur'an. Muslims believe the book was sent by God through the angel Gabriel to the prophet Muhammad. Additional teachings are also recorded in the Hadith.

The foundational belief of Islam is the monotheistic view that God is one. In Arabic, God is called *Allah*. The name Allah was used before the time of Muhammad and does not specify any gender. Because Islam teaches the unity of God, Muslims reject the

Christian doctrine of the Trinity. Muslims also reject the Eastern religions that teach polytheism.

If we want to understand the history and theology of Islam, we must first study its founder. Muhammad is not only the founder of Islam, but his life and example set the pattern for how Muslims are to live.

Who is Muhammad?

Islam began in the early seventh century by Muhammad ibn Abdullah ibn Abd al-Muttalib.[1] He was born in 570 into the Quraysh tribe that had the responsibility of maintaining the Ka'bah (a stone used in pagan rituals in Mecca).

Muhammad's father died almost six months before he was born, and his mother died when he was six years old. So Muhammad was reared by his grandfather, who died when he was eight. Finally, his uncle became his custodian. During his teen years he followed his uncle on trips to Syria to trade goods. Overall, Muhammad lived a normal life, except that he never participated in the pagan rituals in Mecca.

After his years of traveling with his uncle, Muhammad became a merchant. As a young man, he obtained the patronage of Khadijah, a wealthy widow merchant who was 15 years his senior. Muhammad led her trade caravans all over the Arabian Peninsula and as far away as Damascus. At age 25 he married her, and they had several children together.

When Muhammad was 40 years of age, he had a vision. Sometimes he would retire to a cave on Mount Hira (outside Mecca) for relaxation. In 610, he claimed to have received a vision from the angel Gabriel during the month of Ramadan. At first he wondered about its source, but his wife Khadijah (and others) believed he was a prophet. After this first revelation, Muhammad did not receive another for nearly three years. During that time, he became despondent and doubted whether Allah was pleased with his conduct.

But then additional revelations came to him, and did so until his death. These messages were later compiled and recorded in the Qur'an. Over time, some of these revelations became more unusual. He claimed to speak to the dead and even prayed for the dead at one cemetery. He also received revelations from both Allah and Satan.[2] Perhaps the most famous of these are the so-called Satanic Verses.

Muhammad began preaching against the greed, economic oppression, and idolatry of his time. He also preached against the polytheism of the Arab tribes and called on the many factions of the Arab peoples to unite under the worship of Allah. Muhammad proclaimed to the people in Mecca that they were worshipping false gods and idols. This preaching was not only controversial, it also began to affect the commercial interests of those who profited from the worship at the Ka'bah in Mecca. Even Muhammad's own tribe turned against him. He and his followers came under persecution.

Although some joined Muhammad, most of the residents in Mecca either ignored him or criticized him. His message was not well received even by his Quraysh brethren. It is at that point that Muhammad became very angry. When even his uncle, Abu Lahab, rejected his message, Muhammad cursed him and his wife in violent language: "May the hands of Abu Lahab perish! May he himself perish! Nothing shall his wealth and gains avail him. He shall be burnt in a flaming fire, and his wife, laden with faggots, shall have a rope of fiber around her neck!" (Sura 111:1-5).

In 620, Muhammad claimed that he experienced a night journey with the angel Gabriel that took him from Mecca to a far land (later Muslims said this was Jerusalem, at the location which today is known as the Dome of the Rock). He also said he traveled to both heaven and hell and spoke with prophets from previous centuries, such as Abraham, Moses, and Jesus. He led them in prayer, then returned to Mecca.

Muhammad's wife and uncle both died in 619, and he married another woman. In the meantime, the leaders in Mecca were growing even more concerned about the influence of Muhammad and his followers. Tensions were rising, and even members of Muhammad's own tribe refused to protect him. Various threats were made against his life, and the city leaders devised a plan to assassinate Muhammad in order to rid their city of him and his small Muslim community. Muhammad and his followers eventually fled from Mecca in 622 to Medina (a small agricultural oasis to the north of Mecca), where a band of tribal warriors accepted Muhammad as a prophet. This flight (known as the *Hijra*) marks the beginning of the Muslim calendar. This is why Muslim dates have the designation AH (After Hijra).

What happened after Muhammad left Mecca?

While in Medina, Muhammad began to organize various aspects of Islam. He proposed that the Muslim holy day would be on Friday so that it would not conflict with the Jewish Sabbath. Originally, Muslims prayed toward Jerusalem, but that was later changed to Mecca. Muhammad also adopted Abraham as the patriarch of the Muslim faith, considering him the father of the Arabs through Ishmael.

Muhammad also established what could be considered the foundational document of Islam. This document declared the community of Muslim believers to be the *umma* and set forth the strictures under which they would live. This brotherhood of believers replaced the brotherhood of the tribes. They were to be governed by the Muslim theocracy in which all institutions were subservient to the religion.

During this time, Muhammad built a mosque in Medina and

established the five pillars of Islam, which exist to this day. These include confession, prayer, almsgiving, fasting, and a pilgrimage.

Muhammad also divided the world into two spheres: *dar al-Islam* ("the house of submission—Islam") and *dar al-Harb* ("the house of war"). The first refers to government by Islamic law and tradition, and the second refers to those outside Muslim rule.

While Muhammad and his fellow Muslims were in Medina, they raided caravans and engaged in a number of battles. Although most of these battles were against those from Mecca who rejected his teaching, some were fought against the Jews. In a battle against the last Jewish tribe in Medina, Muhammad and his army killed over 600 Jewish men and took the wives and children as booty.

> "Muhammad, it will be recalled, was not only a prophet and a teacher, like the founders of other religions; he was also the head of a polity and of a community, a ruler and a soldier."[3]
>
> —**Bernard Lewis,** professor and leading authority on Islam

Because Muhammad was raiding caravans from Mecca, relations between Mecca and Muhammad grew worse. After Muhammad raided a Meccan caravan in 624, the leaders of Mecca decided to send an army to Medina to defeat Muhammad and his followers.

This was a major turning point in the life of Muhammad, in what is now called the Battle of Badr. Even though Muhammad's troops were outnumbered three to one, they were able to defeat the Quraysh. This was interpreted as a divine authentication of the blessing of Allah on the teaching of Muhammad. Muhammad also attributed the victory to Allah sending angels. He then said that similar help would come to Muslims who remained faithful to Allah.

> Allah had helped you at Badr, when ye were a contempt-ible little force; then fear Allah: thus may you show your

gratitude. Remember thou saidst to the Faithful: "Is it not enough for you that Allah should help you with three thousand angels specially sent down?" Yes, if ye remain firm, and act aright, even if the enemy should rush here on you in hot haste, your Lord would help you with five thousand angels making a terrific onslaught (Sura 3:123-125).

The victory at Badr also posed a problem: what to do with the spoils of war. One of the chapters of the Qur'an actually spells out the distribution of this booty:

Know that whatever ye take as spoils of war, lo! a fifth thereof is for Allah, and for the messenger and for the kinsman (who hath need) and orphans and the needy and the wayfarer, if ye believe in Allah and that which We revealed unto Our slave on the Day of Discrimination, that day when the two armies met (Sura 8:41).

By 628, the Muslim army was so strong that Muhammad decided to return to Mecca as a pilgrim. Even though he was not allowed to finish his pilgrimage, he did sign a treaty that would allow Muslims to make a pilgrimage to Mecca the next year.

In 630, Muhammad assembled an army of 10,000 men and returned to Mecca and took the city without much bloodshed. Most of the Meccans converted to Islam, and others saw the wisdom of not resisting this new powerful religious and military leader. Four people were executed, including a woman who wrote satirical lyrics about Muhammad. Muhammad demanded a pledge of allegiance from the citizens of Mecca to him and his religion. He also destroyed the idols in the shrine in Mecca (known as the Ka'bah) and instituted the practices of Islam in Mecca.

Muhammad now had control of both Medina and Mecca,

which was the economic and religious center of the Arabian Peninsula. He then decided to return to Medina, a city that came to be known as the City of the Prophet. And he continued to expand his sphere of political and religious influence in the Arabian Peninsula for the next two years. He died in 632 at the pinnacle of his power. That did not bring an end to Islam; instead, the religion began an incredible expansion both to the east to Persia and to the west through northern Africa and into Spain.

Did Muhammad condone assassinations done in his name?

One Muslim historian who wrote a biography of Muhammad mentions that Muhammad ordered the assassinations of people who opposed him. The first person whom he had assassinated was an elderly Jewish man. Muhammad asked, "Who will rid me of Ibnu'l Ashraf?" One of his followers responded, "I will deal with him for you. O apostle of God. I will kill him." Muhammad gave his blessing, but later this follower returned to Muhammad and said that in order to kill this man, he would have to lie. Again, Muhammad gave his follower his blessing. So this follower and a few other Muslims tricked the man into leaving his house so they could kill him with daggers and swords. The account concludes with the statement that "our attack upon God's enemy cast terror among the Jews, and there was no Jew in Medina who did not fear for his life."[4]

Another story in the same biography describes what took place with three Jewish tribes around the city of Medina. Muhammad had portrayed himself as the final prophet in a long line of biblical prophets, and therefore hoped that these Jewish tribes would accept him as a prophet of God. They rejected him and his teaching. He responded by exiling two of the tribes and exercising severe judgment against the third tribe. He called for every man in that tribe to be beheaded. Then his followers were to take the women, children, and property. According to history, somewhere between 600 to 900 Jewish men were ordered beheaded by Muhammad.

Another incident developed when Muhammad and his army captured a town and discovered there was a treasure hidden somewhere in the town. They were convinced that one specific man they had captured knew where it was located, and decided to torture him. Muhammad's men "kindled a fire with flint and steel on his chest until he was nearly dead." When the man still did not reveal the treasure's location, he was beheaded.[5]

Muhammad also ordered the death of his own uncle, Abu Sufyan, who was the leader of a tribe that opposed Muhammad. Although the assassins failed to kill his uncle, when they were returning to Medina they killed a one-eyed shepherd. One of the assassins waited until the man was

> asleep and snoring. I got up and killed him in a more horrible way than any man has been killed. I put the end of my bow in his sound eye. Then I bore down on it until I forced it out at the back of his neck…When I got to Medina…the apostle asked my news and when I told him what had happened, he blessed me.[6]

People who dared to criticize Muhammad were targeted for assassination. A man named Abu Afak showed his disapproval of Muhammad through composing a poem. Muhammad asked, "Who will deal with this rascal for me?" One of his followers volunteered and killed him.[7] After this assassination, a woman wrote a poem against Muhammad that criticized his actions. "When the Apostle heard what she had said, he said 'Who will rid me of Marwan's daughter?'" One of his followers heard him and went to her home that night and killed her. "In the morning he came to the apostle and told him what he had done, and he said, 'You have helped God and His Apostle, O Umayr.'"[8]

What happened after Muhammad's death?

When Muhammad died, his Muslim followers faced a challenge. Who would lead them? Should they choose one person to lead them, or should they separate into many communities? Who would be their spokesman?

Some of Muhammad's Muslim leaders picked Abu Bakr, who was Muhammad's father-in-law and an early supporter. He was chosen to assume the role of caliph or successor to Muhammad. However, some of the followers refused to submit to the leadership of Abu Bakr. Several tribes wanted political independence, and some sought to break away religiously as well. The result was what have come to be known as the Wars of Apostasy. After two years of fighting to put down both religious and political threats, Abu Bakr extended his control over the entire Arabian Peninsula. Islam now had a large standing army of believers and was in a position to extend its influence beyond Arabia.

The leaders who emerged from this period were known as caliphs. The first four caliphs had been companions of Muhammad. During this same period, Muslim armies began to conquer the Persian Empire to the east and began to take control of the North African and Syrian territories of the Byzantine Empire. In a fairly short period of time, Islam was transformed from a religion of a small city-state in the Arabian Peninsula into a major world religion that covered the land from northwest Africa to central Asia.

The third caliph, Uthman, was responsible for collecting the variant versions of the Qur'an. He was murdered by troops who mutinied over matters of pay and privileges. These troops, and others in Medina, declared the new caliph to be Ali, a cousin of Muhammad who was an early convert and also the husband of Muhammad's daughter.

This led to a split that created the two major groups in Islam: Sunni and Shi'ite. The Shi'ite Muslim tradition believes that

Muhammad designated Ali as his successor. This conflict between Ali's supporters and other Muslims was briefly resolved by a Muslim council, but then civil war broke out again between various Muslim factions. When Ali was killed in 661, most Muslims accepted the leadership of one of the caliphs, but the division between the two sects of Islam was now established. Even during the civil wars that took place between them, the world of Islam continued to expand and dominate the region. In many ways, this new Muslim state became the successor to the empires of Rome and Persia. Muslim rule spanned from Spain in the west to India in the east. In the centuries that followed, Islam penetrated deeper into Africa and Asia, extending as far as the Philippines.

This time period was the beginning of the golden age of Islam, which produced some of the world's finest philosophers and mathematicians. Baghdad, for example, had a library unmatched by any other in the world and housed writings from Plato and Aristotle.

Also during this time, conflict between Islam and Christianity erupted. In 691, the Dome of the Rock mosque was erected in

> "For the first thousand years Islam was advancing, Christendom is in retreat and under threat. The new faith conquered the old Christian lands of the Levant and North Africa, and invaded Europe, ruling for a while in Sicily, Spain, Portugal, and even parts of France.... For the past three hundred years, since the failure of the second Turkish siege of Vienna in 1683 and the rise of the European colonial empires in Asia and Africa, Islam has been on the defensive, and the Christian and post-Christian civilization of Europe and her daughters has brought the whole world, including Islam, within its orbit."[9]
>
> —**Bernard Lewis,** professor and leading authority on Islam

Jerusalem. In 715 the Great Mosque was built in Damascus. By 1095, a series of battles were begun in an effort to reclaim the Holy Land from the Muslims.

By the tenth century, the power of the caliphs was reduced as power shifted to the military commanders, who frequently took the title of *sultan* (meaning "authority"). Much of this military leadership was Turkish.

From the tenth to the sixteenth centuries, the size of the Muslim world nearly doubled. This expansion was not so much due to military conquest as it was to traveling merchants and itinerant preachers.

From the sixteenth century onward, Islam began to be affected by the influence of European powers. Eventually much of the Muslim world was colonized by European countries. This situation remained relatively unchanged until the end of World War II. Then many of the Muslim countries gained political independence. The discovery and development of the vast oil reserves in many Muslim lands also brought economic independence. Today, Islam is a dominant influence not only in the Arab world but in many countries around the globe.

THE STRUCTURE OF ISLAM

ISLAM INVOLVES BOTH BELIEFS (basic doctrine) and duties (the five pillars of Islam). A faithful Muslim must both believe and act according to the revelation given in the Qur'an. He or she is to do this as an act of submission to the will of Allah. After all, the word *Islam* means "submission," and the word *Muslim* describes "one who submits."

To understand Islam, one must first understand the basic beliefs and duties of Islam. While it is true that not all Muslims believe the same things, there is a set of foundational beliefs and practices that can be found within every Muslim community. A faithful Muslim must incorporate correct teaching and correct behavior within his or her obedience to Allah.

CORRECT TEACHING

What are the basic beliefs of Islam?

(C) BELIEF

The beliefs of Muslims worldwide are quite diverse, but there are six basic articles of faith common to nearly all Muslims.

The first basic belief is that there is no God but Allah. Before Muhammad came on the scene, the Arabs in the region where he lived were polytheists. Muhammad taught that they should devote themselves solely to the chief God of the pantheon, whose name was Allah. To worship any other deity is considered *shirk,* or blasphemy.

2   The second article of faith is a belief in angels and jinn. The Muslim belief in angels is in many ways similar to the Christian belief. According to Islam, two angels are believed to accompany every Muslim—one on the right to record his good deeds, and one on the left to record his evil deeds. Jinn are not the same as demons. Rather, jinn are spirit beings capable of both good and evil actions. They also have the ability to take possession of human beings.

3   The third article is belief in God's holy books. There are 104 holy books mentioned in the Qur'an. The major books include the Law given to Moses, the Psalms given to David, the Gospel (or *Injil*) given to Jesus, and the Qur'an given to Muhammad. Islam teaches that each of these books communicate the same basic message of God's will to man. But even a cursory reading of these will find major discrepancies between the Bible and the Qur'an. Islam teaches that these differences arose because the Bible has been corrupted through the ages in its transmission to us.

4   Muslims also believe in a number of God's prophets. While they believe there were many prophets, there is no agreement as to how many prophets there have been. Some writers say that there were hundreds of thousands of prophets. Among those who are considered prophets are Adam, Noah, Abraham, Moses, and Jesus. All Muslims agree that Muhammad was God's final and supreme prophet. He is referred to as the "seal" of the prophets (Sura 33:40). Though Muhammad even wrote in the Qur'an that he was a sinner, there are still Muslims throughout the world who hold him in very high esteem, and some even come close to worshipping him.

5   Predestination is a fifth article of faith. A frequent expression among Muslims is *inshallah,* which means, "if Allah wills." This is essentially a belief in predestination (*qadar*). Allah is the sovereign

ruler of the universe, and whatever he wills comes to pass. Allah is directing the fate of each individual according to his divine will.

Although some Muslims have modified this doctrine of predestination in their teachings, the Qur'an appears to support the idea that all things (both good and evil) are the direct result of God's will. Those who conclude that Islam is a fatalistic religion have good reasons for doing so.

On the other hand, the Qur'an also teaches that believers are to follow the straight path (Sura 1:6). Therefore, they are responsible for their actions. They must do what Allah commands in order to please him and be admitted into paradise. Muslims must obey the five pillars of Islam in order to attain this reward.

The final article of faith is belief in a final judgment. According (6) to Islam, Allah will judge the works of all men at the end of history. Those whose good deeds outweigh their bad deeds will enter into *works* paradise. All others will be consigned to hell. Essentially Islam is a works-oriented religion in which a person's good works becomes the means to salvation.

What are the five pillars of Islam? *CORRECT BEHAVIOR*

Although the beliefs of Muslims vary, all agree on what are called the five pillars of Islam. These provide an accurate summary of the practices of this religion.

1. *Shahadah:* The first pillar is recitation of the creed, "There is no God but Allah, and Muhammad is the prophet of Allah." This creed is found in many passages within the Qur'an (Sura 3:81; 5:83-84; 2:255; 3:18; 3:144; 4:87; 7:172; 33:40; 48:29; 64:8).

This statement is the foundation for all other beliefs in Islam. It is what makes someone a Muslim. These words are whispered into the ears of a Muslim both at birth and at death. Muslims repeat the Shahadah in prayer (spoken 14 times a day in the ritual prayers).

Those who convert to Islam must recite the creed; it is generally believed you must recite this creed in the presence of two witnesses in order to formally convert to Islam. But conversion involves more than merely intellectual assent to the creed. The devout Muslim must unite belief (*imam*) with practice (*din*).

2. *Salat:* The second pillar is the daily practice of prayer. Muslim prayers are vocal, orderly, and directional. They may be done individually or in community, but they are required to be done five times each day.

The daily prayers must be voiced in Arabic as the follower of Islam faces toward Mecca. Words and gestures are specific as Muslims line up in orderly rows (Sura 2:3,117; 11:114; 17:78; 20:14,130; 30:17-18). Men and women are segregated within the mosque. A Muslim stands and kneels during prayer, and these actions are called *rakahs.*

The central prayer for Muslims is the *Fatiha,* which many have compared to the Lord's Prayer in Christianity. It is said out loud during the daily times of prayer, as well as on special occasions: "In the name of Allah, Most Gracious, Most Merciful. Praise be to Allah the Cherisher and Sustainer of the Worlds. Most Gracious, Most Merciful; Master of the Day of Judgment. Thee do we worship, and Thine aid we seek. Show us the straight path" (Sura 1:1-6).

In Muslim and Western countries where there is a mosque, a prayer leader climbs to the top of the minaret in the mosque and calls the believers to prayer. He chants in Arabic, "God is great. There is no god but Allah, and Muhammad is the messenger of Allah. Come to prayer. Come to prayer. Come to success in this life and the hereafter." Within the mosque, there is water for absolution. Before they pray, Muslims wash their hands, forearms, face, and feet. They also clean their noses and rinse their mouths.

3. *Zakat:* The third pillar is almsgiving, which is mandated giving to the poor and needy within society (Sura 2:43,83,110,177,277;

9:60; 103; 24:56; 27:3; 57:7; 59:7; 98:5). Being an orphan himself, Muhammad was deeply concerned for the needy. A Muslim must first recognize that everything is the property of Allah. The Qur'an requires that each Muslim give 2.5 percent of one's income to the poor or to the spread of Islam. The collected funds are used for building and supporting mosques, for printing the Qur'an, and for the advancement of Islam.

4. *Sawm:* The fourth pillar of Islam is the fast during the month of Ramadan (Sura 2:183-185). This is during the ninth lunar month of the Muslim calendar. This is a significant date in the Muslim calendar for two reasons. First, this is the time when Muhammad is said to have received the first of his revelations from God. And second, it is the time when he and his followers made their historic trek from Mecca to Medina.

During this month, Muslims in good health are required to abstain from all food, drink, smoking, and sexual intercourse during daylight hours. Instead, Muslims are to read the Qur'an meditatively and introspectively. The Qur'an has been divided into 30 equal parts for reading during this time. This monthlong fast promotes the Muslim's self-discipline, dependence on Allah, and compassion for the needy. The festival of Id Fitr (breaking the fast) is held at the end of Ramadan as a time of celebration for adhering to the fast. This includes visitations, meetings, and meals.

5. *Hajj:* The fifth pillar is a pilgrimage to Mecca that occurs during the last month of the Muslim year. Every able-bodied Muslim is to make this pilgrimage at least once during his life (Sura 2:196-201; 3:97; 22:26-29). Only Muslims may enter Mecca, which is the holiest city in Islam and the birthplace of Muhammad.

The focal point of Mecca is the Ka'bah, which is an ancient stone building 30 feet wide and 40 feet long. A black stone (believed to be a meteorite) is set in the corner. The Ka'bah existed before the time of Muhammad. He taught that the people's worship had been corrupted and removed 360 idols from the Ka'bah and instituted the worship of Allah in their place.

Those who make the pilgrimage must circle the Ka'bah seven times, run seven times between the two hills of Mecca, travel 13 miles to the place where Muhammad preached his last sermon, then go to another site to throw seven stones at the devil. Many of the elements of this prescribed activity predate Islam and are of pagan origin.

Is there a sixth pillar of Islam?

Many Muslims believe Islam actually has six pillars. That sixth pillar is jihad. There are over 100 verses in the Qur'an that call upon Muslims to engage in jihad.

The word *jihad* is actually the noun form of the Arabic verb *jahidi*, which means "to strive hard." This verse is an example: "O Prophet! Strive hard against the unbelievers and the hypocrites, and be firm against them. Their abode is Hell, and evil refuge indeed" (Sura 9:73).

Although some Muslims understand this striving to be intellectual and philosophical in nature, the usual translation of *jihad* involves a holy war. That has been the traditional interpretation since the time of Muhammad.

Bernard Lewis, a professor of Near Eastern studies at Princeton University and a leading authority on Islam, says that "the more common interpretation, and that of the overwhelming majority of the classical jurists and commentators, presents jihad as armed struggle for Islam against infidels and apostates."[1]

According to the Qur'an, jihad is to be waged on the battlefield: "When you meet the unbelievers in the battlefield, strike off their heads and, when you have laid them low, bind your captives firmly" (Sura 47:4).

Another passage concerning jihad is this: "O ye who believe!

Fight the unbelievers who gird you about, and let them find firmness in you; and know that Allah is with those who fear Him" (Sura 9:123).

Muslims are also to wage jihad not only against unbelievers but against those who have strayed from the faith: "Prophet, make war on the unbelievers and the hypocrites and deal rigorously with them. Hell shall be their home: and evil fate" (Sura 9:73).

Ultimately, Muslims believe they are fighting against Satan and his allies: "Those who believe fight in the cause of Allah, and those who reject faith fight in the cause of evil: so fight ye against the friends of Satan" (Sura 4:76).

Point of View: "Let's define the term *jihad*. It could even be considered the sixth pillar of Islam, but the Sufis [a sect of Islam] later developed a concept of greater jihad that is kind of this intellectual struggle. So I guess how you define that term determines whether or not you are talking about a peaceful neighbor of someone that you might be concerned about."

Spencer: "*Jihad*, in Arabic, means 'struggle,' very simply. There are many kinds of struggles identified in the Islamic tradition. Right now in the Islamic republic of Iran, they have the government level also known as the Department of Agricultural Jihad. And that doesn't have anything to do with war, obviously. It just has to do with trying to increase yields on farmland. So, jihad, as such, does not necessarily have anything to do with waging war.

"However, there is an unmistakable tradition within Islam that goes back to the Qur'an and the example of Muhammad himself that does define the struggle as being warfare against unbelievers in order to establish Islamic law as supreme. This is something that has been pursued by Muslims throughout history and is being pursued today by the jihad terrorists."

—Interview with Robert Spencer on *Point of View* radio talk show[2]

Are verses about jihad in the Qur'an taken out of context?

I have found that when verses about the sword are quoted from the Qur'an, skeptics wonder if these are just a few isolated passages or if they have been quoted out of context. How can we answer this question?

First, the passages about jihad are found throughout the Qur'an. In fact, there are over 100 verses that advocate jihad. Many of them are found in Sura 9. This was the last chapter communicated by Muhammad, and illustrates his desire to use the sword and other forms of violence to spread the religion of Islam.

Second, let's consider the contexts. While some will argue that these verses were intended only for the time of Muhammad, there is nothing within the Qur'an that justifies such an interpretation. Nowhere within the Qur'an do we find such a restriction placed on these verses of the sword.

Third, these passages are used today by Muslim leaders who advocate jihad warfare and call upon followers to engage in warfare, terrorism, assassination, or the persecution of unbelievers. Osama bin Laden quotes from Sura 9:14 ("Fight them, and Allah will punish them by your hands, cover them with shame") in a videotape found in Afghanistan by the U.S. Army.

"[T]he history of Islam has essentially been a history of conquest and reconquest. The seventh-century 'breakout' of Islam from Arabia was followed by the rapid conquest of North Africa, the invasion and virtual conquest of Spain, and a thrust into France that carried the crescent to the gates of Paris."[3]

—Paul Johnson

Is jihad taught only in the Qur'an?

While the Qur'an is the foundational book in Islam, there is also the Hadith. It is a collection of the sayings of Muhammad and is considered the second-most important book in Islam. From the Hadith we can gain additional perspective on jihad. Here are four examples:

- "Allah's apostle said, 'Know that paradise is under the shades of swords'" (Hadith 4:55).

- "Allah's apostle said, 'I have been ordered to fight with the people till they say, "None has the right to be worshipped but Allah," and whoever says, "None has the right to be worshipped but Allah," his life and property will be saved by men'" (Hadith 4:125).

- "It is not fitting for a prophet that he should have prisoners of war [and free them with ransom] until he has made a great slaughter [among his enemies] in the land" (Hadith 4:161).

- "Whoever changed his Islamic religion, then kill him" (Hadith 9:45).

Does the Qur'an support the martyrdom of suicide bombers?

In Islam, a martyr is called a *shaheed* ("witness"). The concept of the shaheed is not found in the Qur'an, but a discussion can be found in the Hadith.

Muslims who die in a holy war (*jihad bis saif*) are usually considered a martyr in Islam. This would be different than dying as a suicide bomber. Some Muslims consider a suicide bomber a martyr, but other Muslims would disagree because there are strict admonitions in Islam against suicide. These Muslims would consider death by suicide bombing contrary to the teachings of Muhammad.

The Qur'an teaches that those who die in a holy war against infidels will be admitted into paradise (Sura 47:4-6) because Allah will not forget their deeds. The Hadith expands upon this and promotes martyrdom and promises rewards in heaven.

What is the psychology of suicide bombers?

Pierre Rehov, a French filmmaker, produced the documentary "Suicide Killers." He was able to uncover some of the psychology of suicide bombers. Here are some observations he made on MSNBC's *Connected Coast to Coast* program:[4]

- "People don't understand the devastating culture behind this unbelievable phenomenon. My film is not politically correct because it addresses the real problem—showing the real face of Islam. It points the finger against a culture of hatred in which the uneducated are brainwashed to a level where their only solution in life becomes to kill themselves and kill others in the name of a God whose word, as transmitted by other men, has become their only certitude."

- "I came to the conclusion that we are facing a neurosis at the level of an entire civilization. Most neuroses have in common a dramatic event, generally linked to an unacceptable sexual behavior. In this case, we are talking of kids living all their lives in pure frustration, with no opportunity to experience sex, love, tenderness or even understanding from the opposite sex."

- "The separation between men and women in Islam is absolute. So is contempt toward women, who are totally dominated by men. This leads to a situation of pure anxiety, in which normal behavior is not possible. It is no coincidence that suicide killers are mostly young men dominated subconsciously by an overwhelming libido that they not only cannot satisfy but are afraid of, as if it is the work of the devil. Since Islam describes heaven as a place where everything on earth will finally be allowed, and promises 72 virgins to those frustrated kids, killing others and killing themselves to reach this redemption becomes their only solution."

What are the major divisions of Islam?

Islam is not a monolithic system. Though all Muslims draw their inspiration from Muhammad and the teachings in the Qur'an, there are many identifiable groups and movements within Islam.

The most significant division is between Sunni and Shi'a Islam. The Sunnis comprise about 80 to 90 percent of all Muslims. They draw their name from the fact that they look both to the Qur'an and to the "Sunna" in establishing proper Muslim conduct. The Sunna is the recorded behavior or example of Muhammad and of the early Muslim community. There are many subdivisions among the Sunnis, but they all identify themselves as Sunni.

Sunnis currently control the holy cities of Mecca and Medina. They adhere to the five pillars of Islam and take a strong stand on the proper successors to Muhammad. They believe the successors must be males from the Quraysh tribe. These leaders are the caliphs who govern Islam and provide theological direction to all Muslims, including the interpretation of sharia law. These caliphs ruled continuously until 1932, when the Ottoman Empire fell.

The other major group of Muslims is the Shi'ites. They comprise about ten percent of all Muslims. They reside mainly in southern Iraq and in Iran. The word *Shi'ite* means "partisan" and refers to the fact that Shi'ites are "partisans of Ali." As we have noted, Ali was the son-in-law and cousin of Muhammad and one of the early caliphs. The Shi'ites say that the leader of Islam should be a descendant of Ali, whom they believe possesses a divine anointing for this task. Ali was not selected as the first caliph, but the fourth. Shi'ites consider him the first *imam.*

When conflicts arose, Ali was killed. His body is buried in Iraq and his grave site is a prominent Shi'ite shrine. According to Shi'ite teaching, pilgrimage to this shrine provides forgiveness for past and present sins.

"Iran's president is not only a devout Shiite Muslim; he is also what is known as a *Mahdaviat.* The term means one who believes in and prepares for the *Mahdi.* The *Mahdi,* also known as the 'Twelfth Imam,' is the Shiite equivalent of a messiah: 'the restorer of religion and justice who will rule before the end of the world.'

"For Ahmadinejad, preparing for the Mahdi has included 'secretly [instructing] the [Tehran] city council to build a grand avenue to prepare for the Mahdi,' the building of a special mosque dedicated to the cult of the Mahdi, and construction of a railroad line to transport pilgrims there."[5]

—**Chuck Colson,** author and commentator

Shi'ites are a majority in only a few Muslim countries (Iran, Iraq, Azerbaijan, and Bahrain). There are various sects of Shi'a, but the main branch is known as the "Twelvers." They believe in 12 imams who linked God and man after Muhammad's death. The first imam was Ali, and the twelfth was Mahdi. According to the Twelvers, Mahdi was taken by God into hiding from his enemies in 870. They also believe that the boy never died and will someday return to earth bringing justice at the end of days. Until his return, Shi'ites believe that an ayatollah may rule in his place. They also believe that the ayatollah is infallible. There have been a number of ayatollahs in the Shi'ite country of Iran.

There are a few other differences between Sunnis and Shi'ites.

For example, the ways in which they hold their hands during prayer. Shiites also commemorate the death of the third imam, Hussein, who was beheaded by the Sunni Army in 680. Some Shi'ite pilgrims visit his shrine, and men dressed in white beat themselves until they bleed as penance for those who left Hussein to be killed.

After the first Gulf War, violence surfaced between Sunnis and Shi'ites in Iraq. The United States encouraged the Shi'ites to rise up against Saddam Hussein and the Sunnis. Hussein retaliated by eradicating entire districts of Shi'ites. Shi'ites believe they have a score to settle with the Sunni minority that oppressed them.

A third group of Muslims are the Sufis. They seek a mystical experience of God rather than a merely intellectual knowledge of Him. They are also given to a number of superstitious practices.

Sufi Muslims are the mystics in Islam. They believe that the soul can rise to Allah during prayer and other spiritual exercises. Although they also read the Qur'an, they read it in a different way than other Muslims. They believe that it is an allegory of our soul's union with Allah. They, therefore, follow an inward path (*tariqa*) in their faith.

The word *sufi* means "purity" and comes from the fact that the first Sufis wore white and withdrew from society to practice an ascetic lifestyle. They use various spiritual exercises in an attempt to experience God directly. Perhaps the best-known example of Sufis would be the "whirling dervishes" who spin around and repeat the name of Allah as they dance.

What is Wahhabism, and how does it affect Saudi Arabia?

Wahhabism is a movement within Sunni Islam that was founded in the eighteenth century by Muhammad ibn 'Abd al-Wahhab, who established a form of Muslim literalism that flourishes today in Saudi Arabia. He and his followers attempted to purify Islam and return it to its Muslim roots and pursued a literal interpretation of the Qur'an. Wahhab aggressively fought for purity within Islam by burning books, destroying Muslim holy places, and killing Muslims who disagreed with him.[6]

The influence of Wahhabism on the Saudis provided a platform for this sect of Islam to gain national and international attention. When Saudi forces conquered Arabia in 1925, they took control of Islam's two most holy cities: Mecca and Medina. This provided them with a strong religious platform because of the annual pilgrimages many Muslims make to Mecca each year.

The oil money of Saudi Arabia has provided a strong financial platform for Wahhabism, which became the "official, state-enforced doctrine of one of the most influential governments in all Islam."[7] This oil money helped to fund the propagation of Wahhabist views at home and abroad.[8]

How influential is Wahhabism? It was the primary influence on Osama bin Laden and all the 9/11 hijackers. It has also influenced the theology of the Taliban in Afghanistan. Bernard Lewis uses this analogy to illustrate the influence of Wahhabism: Imagine that the Ku Klux Klan or a similar group took control of Texas and its oil. Then imagine what they could do with the money earned from this oil to propagate their version of "Christianity" through heavily endowed schools and colleges.[9]

During the Soviet occupation of Afghanistan in the 1980s, the Wahhabi soldiers fought the Soviets, with U.S. support. There, the Wahhabis linked with radical followers of Sayyid Qutb. One commentator said this alliance was like "mixing nitroglycerin in a blender."[10] The result was a more militant strain of Wahhabism that has an emphasis on taking the fight to outsiders (e.g., the infidels and the West).[11]

What do black Muslims believe, and are they part of Islam?

Although other Muslims do not regard black Muslims as

orthodox, they do have a following, especially in the United States. The Nation of Islam began in the black community in the 1930s through Elijah Poole, who later changed his name to Elijah Muhammad. The beliefs range from Islamic theology to occult mysticism to racist concepts. Black Muslims accept the Qur'an and believe that Allah is God. They also teach that Christianity is the white man's religion.

Black Muslims believe that the black man was the original creation and that God will ultimately have the black man rule when the white man is eliminated. Elijah's original dream was for his followers to have a land of their own (either outside the United States or in the southern part of the nation).

In the 1960s, a division arose within the Nation of Islam. Malcolm X began to gain a following. He called for a closer affiliation with the orthodox teachings of Islam and was critical of the marital infidelities of Elijah Muhammad, whose followers assassinated Malcolm X in 1965.

The current leader of the Nation of Islam is Louis Farrakhan. He has continued many of the teachings of Elijah Muhammad and is probably best known for organizing the Million Man March in Washington, DC.

What is the significance of Mecca?

Mecca is the holiest city within the religion of Islam and is the place where the Sacred Mosque (*al-Masjid al-Haram*) is located. In fact, Mecca is considered so holy that non-Muslims are not permitted to enter the city. It is considered holy because it is the birthplace of Muhammad and the place where he first began to teach from his recitations (the Qur'an).

The Qur'an also teaches that Mecca is the place where Abraham was told to sacrifice Ishmael. This teaching is contrary to the biblical teaching that Abraham was to sacrifice Isaac on Mount Moriah.

Mecca is also the object of every Muslim's prayer. Each day, over one billion Muslims pray five times in the direction of Mecca. All able-bodied Muslims who can afford to go are commanded to make a pilgrimage at least once during their lifetime.

What do Muslims do in Mecca?

The Ka'bah is a small cubical building within the Sacred Mosque. Muslims claim that Abraham built the Ka'bah. Even before the birth of Muhammad, religious activities took place at the Ka'bah, which had been a shrine and trading center for many generations. When Muhammad returned to Mecca, he removed the religious idols from the Ka'bah and dedicated it as the center of worship to Allah.

Muslims gather for their pilgrimage to Mecca (known as the *hajj*) during the month of Dhu al-Hijjah. The primary focus is the Ka'bah. While they are there, pilgrims must circle the Ka'bah seven times. As they do this, many try to kiss or touch the Ka'bah's cornerstone.

Pilgrims also drink from the well of Zamzam and often bring back a bottle of water from this well. The water supposedly has special properties and health benefits.

They also travel to a small village in which there are stone columns that symbolize the devil. They throw stones at these columns. They also travel to the Hill of Arafat for prayer. This is the traditional site of Muhammad's farewell sermon.

THE THEOLOGY OF ISLAM

THE BASIC THEOLOGY OF ISLAM is found within the Qur'an, which is the foundational religious text of Islam. The first thing a Muslim hears at birth and the last thing a Muslim hears at death are the words of the Qur'an.

Islam teaches that the Qur'an contains the words of Allah, and the "mother of the book" is actually in heaven with Allah (Sura 13:39; 43:3-4; 85:21-23). It is composed of revelations given to Muhammad over a 23-year period and was later compiled during the years 646–650 from materials written by Muhammad before his death in 632. Muslims regard the Qur'an as Allah's final revelation to mankind.

To understand Islam, you must understand what the Qur'an teaches about God, Muhammad, Jesus, and the prophets. Moreover, you must also learn what the Qur'an teaches about such important issues as sin and salvation.

What are the scriptures of Islam?

The Arabic word *Qur'an* is the noun form of the Arabic verb *qara'a*, which means "to recite." Muhammad said that when the angel Gabriel appeared to him, he was commanded three separate times to "recite." Sura 12:2 says, "We have sent it down as an Arabic Qur'an, in order that ye may learn wisdom." The Qur'an is the collection of those recitations revealed to Muhammad in Arabic. Muslims believe that the only way to understand the revelation in the Qur'an is in the original Arabic language. For that reason, an English translation of the Qur'an is seen as merely an interpretation and not a real Qur'an. The English-language translations may be helpful for personal use, but they have no weight in any religious debate or discussion.

The Qur'an consists of 114 chapters (or suras) that include 6,616 verses (ayas). Of these chapters, 86 were written in Mecca and 28 were written in Medina. The Qur'an is about one-third the size of the Bible. Also, the text of the Qur'an is not in chronological order. With the exception of the first chapter, the rest of the chapters are arranged by length with the longest chapters first. As it turns out, the Qur'an is almost in reverse chronological order. That has caused some to suggest that it could be read from back to front in order to understand the progression of the revelation.

Like the Bible, the Qur'an claims to be divine inspiration. Islam teaches that the Qur'an is a word-for-word copy of God's final revelation supposedly sent down from heaven during the month of Ramadan, during the night of power (Sura 17:85). This revelation was supposedly revealed to Muhammad through the angel Gabriel (Sura 25:32).

Muslims believe that the Qur'an was divinely revealed in its present state without corruption. Thus, Islam does not allow literary or historical criticism of the Qur'an. In essence, the Qur'an is to be read and memorized, but not to be questioned (Sura 5:101).

Muslims show great respect to the Qur'an because they consider it to be the perfect revelation from Allah. Among the ways they show their reverence is by kissing the book and touching it to their forehead. And they will also store the Qur'an in the highest shelf in their house.

The transmission of the Qur'an was a fairly simple process. After Muhammad's death, Caliph Abu Bakr collected the recitations into one document, based upon the memorization of Muhammad's companions. Later, in 652, Caliph Uthman established the authorized version of the Qur'an and burned all earlier conflicting versions.

In addition to the Qur'an there is the Hadith, which provides a narration of Muhammad's life and is important in determining the Sunnah, or Muslim way of life. The Hadith is a collection of: (1) what Muhammad said (*qawl*), (2) what Muhammad did (*fi'l*), and (3) what Muhammad approved (*taqrir*). These passages provide guidance in how Muslims are to live and behave. Muhammad is the example every faithful Muslim is to follow.

How does the Qur'an view the Bible?

A foundational belief in Islam is that mankind can often be led astray and that humans can be forgetful about God. So Muhammad taught that God sent various prophets (such as Moses and Jesus) to bring fresh revelation to humanity.

However, Muhammad also taught that these various revelations have been lost or corrupted. While most Muslims profess respect for the Bible, they also believe that the Bible has been corrupted in the course of transmission. Only the Qur'an, they believe, has been perfectly transmitted to this day. It is the authentic and authoritative word from Allah.

Both the Bible and the Qur'an claim to be divine revelation, and both books claim to have been accurately preserved through the centuries. But Islam is very insistent about the preservation of the Qur'an. For example, if you tour an Islamic center, the guide will tell you that the current copy of the Qur'an contains the exact words given by Muhammad to his followers, with absolutely no mistakes.

By contrast, Christians do not make quite the same sweeping

claim regarding the Bible. While they do affirm that the original manuscripts of the Bible were without error, they do not claim the text has been transmitted perfectly through the ages. They believe that the transmission of Scripture has been extremely accurate, but will not go so far as to make a claim similar to what many Muslims say about the Qur'an.

The Bible and the Qur'an disagree with one another on major issues. The two books make contradictory claims about God, Jesus, salvation, and biblical history. Both sets of claims cannot be true because the accounts contradict each other.

Islam solves this dilemma by teaching that the Jews and Christians corrupted the Bible. This is the doctrine of *tahrif,* which is the Arabic word for "corruption." That is Islam's explanation for why the Qur'an and the Bible disagree—the Bible has been corrupted by the People of the Book.

There is a problem with this view: The Qur'an says many positive and complimentary things about the Bible. For example, Sura 5:44 says, "It was we who revealed the Law to Moses; therein was guidance and light." Verse 46 goes on to say, "And in their footsteps We sent Jesus the son of Mary, confirming the Law that has come before him. We sent him the Gospel: therein was guidance and light."

The Qur'an (5:68) has this to say about Jews and Christians: "Say, O People of the Book! Ye have not ground to stand upon unless you stand fast by the Law, the Gospel, and all the revelation that has come to you from your Lord."

Allah tells Muhammad to consider previous revelation (10:94) to Jews and Christians: "If thou wert in doubt as to what we have revealed unto thee, then ask those who have been reading the Book from before thee." It also says in Sura 29:46, "And dispute ye not with the People of the Book, except with means better."

It is important to note that in the early days of Islam, the Bible was held in higher esteem than it is today. Muhammad taught that his revelation was the culmination of other revelation provided by such prophets as Moses and Jesus. Therefore, he encouraged his followers to read and learn from these previous revelations. Only later did Muslims begin to teach the Bible was corrupt.

Consider the logical problem this creates. Though the Qur'an calls the Bible the "word of God" (Sura 6:115), Muslims argue that the Old and New Testaments have been corrupted and contend that a lost gospel of Jesus has been replaced with Matthew, Mark, Luke, and John.

Here are the problems with this perspective: First, the Qur'an calls the Bible the word of God, and acknowledges that it is divine revelation. Second, the Qur'an teaches that Jesus was a prophet and that his teaching had authority. Finally, Muhammad told Muslims to go to Christians (who had been reading the Bible) to affirm Muhammad's message (Sura 10:94).

Therefore, it appears that Muhammad believed that the Bible in existence in the seventh century was accurate. And the Bible we have in our hands today is the same Bible that existed in the seventh century. So if the Bible in Muhammad's time was accurate, why don't Muslims consider today's copy also accurate?

Also, the Qur'an does, in fact, suffer from textual omissions and even errors. From the time of the death of Muhammad to the time during which the Qur'an was compiled, some of what Muhammad spoke was lost due to the deaths of his companions, who had memorized specific passages. And later, when multiple versions of the Qur'an appeared, there was a great controversy among Muslims about which version was accurate. The Caliph Uthman ordered Zaid bin Thabit to collect all the copies in use, create a standard version, and destroy the rest.[1]

How do the Bible and the Qur'an contradict each other?

Here are just a few examples:

- The Qur'an teaches that Christians worship three gods: the Father, the Mother (Mary), and the Son (Jesus) (Sura 5:116). But the Bible teaches there is one God in three persons (the Trinity).

- The Qur'an says that Abraham was told to sacrifice Ishmael (Sura 37:100-111), while the Bible teaches that Abraham was told to sacrifice Isaac.

- The Qur'an teaches that Jesus was not crucified (Sura 4:157). The Bible teaches Jesus Christ was crucified on a cross.

Many of the statements in the Qur'an are at odds with historical facts that can be verified through documented accounts.

- The Qur'an says that the Samaritans tricked the Israelites at the exodus and were the ones who built the golden calf (Sura 20:85-9x7). For the record, the word *Samaritan* didn't even exist until 722 B.C., and is several hundred years after the exodus.

- The Qur'an also states that Alexander the Great was a Muslim who worshiped Allah (Sura 18:89-98). But Alexander lived from 356 B.C. to 323 B.C., or hundreds of years *before* Muhammad proclaimed the revelation in Sura 18:89-98.

What is the basis for Islamic monotheism?

Islam is a monotheistic religion. It teaches, "There is no God but Allah, and Muhammad is the prophet of Allah." This creed is a statement of faith that is routinely heard from the lips of every faithful Muslim. It the creed by which every Muslim is called to prayer five times a day.

Allah is the name of God in Islam. And it is important to note that this name for God was known even before the beginning of Islam. In fact, Muhammad's father bore the name Abd-Allah. Before the time of Muhammad, the tribes in the Arabian Peninsula worshipped many gods. Muhammad, however, taught that there was one true God. *Allah* literally means "the God." He is one and transcendent. Muhammad proclaimed that all the other deities that were worshiped at the time were not worthy of worship as divine beings.

The Qur'an provides the identity and character of Allah. The first chapter of the Qur'an is known as the *Faitha,* or "opening." It summarizes the foundational beliefs of Muslims about Allah. According to the passage, he is most gracious and merciful, the sustainer of the world, and master of the Day of Judgment. Therefore, he is to be worshipped (Sura 1:1-7). And in one chapter near the end of the Qur'an, we read, "He is God, One, God the Everlasting Refuge, who has not begotten, and has not been begotten, and equal to Him is not any one" (Sura 112).

This passage (along with others in the Qur'an) teaches the absolute unity and sovereignty of Allah. The oneness of God precludes any plural nature to God. And there is no equal to Allah. He is the only God in the heavens, and therefore the only deity worth worshipping and obeying.

The Qur'an teaches that evidence of Allah can be found in creation. There are over 80 passages in the Qur'an that describe the wonders of nature. These all point to the existence of a God who created the heavens and earth. In fact, the Qur'an teaches that we can use logic and reason to determine that God exists because He has manifested Himself through His creation (Sura 45:3-4).

The Qur'an also teaches that creation provides theological arguments for the existence of God and the falsity of other deities. Here are a few examples:

- God is united to His creation (Sura 6:96-100).

- Polytheism and atheism are contrary to reason (Sura 23:119).

- Dualism is self-destructive (Sura 21:22).

Because of the Qur'an's strong emphasis on monotheism, Muslims reject the idea that God could be more than one person or that God could have a partner. The Qur'an teaches the unity of God (*tawhid*). Allah is one God and the same God for all people. Anyone who does not believe this is guilty of the sin of *shirk*—this is the quintessential sin in Islam (Sura 4:48). According to Islam, God cannot have a partner and cannot be joined together in the Godhead with other persons. Muslims, therefore, reject the Christian idea of the Trinity.

Muslims also differ from Christians in their understanding of the nature and character of God. The God of the Bible is knowable. Jesus came into the world that we might know God (John 17:3).

Islam teaches a very different view of God. Allah is transcendent and distant. He is separate from His creation. He is exalted and far removed from mankind. While we may know His will, we cannot know Him personally. In fact, there is very little written about the character of God. Allah is the creator and sustainer of the creation, but He is also unknowable. No person can ever personally know and have a relationship with Allah. Instead, humans are to live in total submission to the will of Allah.

Moreover, Allah does not personally enter into human history. Instead, he deals with the world through His word (the Qur'an), through His prophets (such as Muhammad), and through angels (such as Gabriel).

If you ask a Muslim to describe Allah, most likely he will recite to you a key passage that lists some of the names of God (Sura 59). The Qur'an requires that God be called by these "beautiful names." This passage describes him as Most Gracious, Most Merciful, The Sovereign, The Holy One, The Guardian of Faith, The Preserver of Safety, The Exalted in Might, etc.

A Muslim will also talk about 99 names of Allah. According to tradition, Muhammad said that to memorize and say these 99 names of God will aid a Muslim in entering paradise. Many Muslims even use prayer beads to help them keep track of the various names of God.

The Muslim perspective on God's love is also very different from the Christian view. Crucial to Christians is the belief that "God so loved the world" (John 3:16).

By contrast, Muslims grow up hearing about all the people Allah does not love:

- "For Allah loves not transgressors" (Sura 2:190).

- "Allah loves not the impious and the sinful" (Sura 2:276).

- "Allah loves not the unbelievers" (Sura 3:32).

- "For Allah loves not the evildoers" (Sura 3:57).

- "Allah loves not the arrogant and boastful men" (Sura 4:36).

What do Muslims believe about Muhammad?

Christians frequently make the mistake of assuming that Muhammad has essentially the same role in Islam that Jesus has in Christianity. This is not true. Muslims see Muhammad as a messenger, while Christians see Jesus as *the* message, or the Word (John 1:1).

Muslims believe that Muhammad was the final prophet from Allah. He is referred to as the "seal of the prophets" (Sura 33:40). But while he is revered as the greatest of the prophets, most do not teach that he was sinless. The Qur'an does not claim that he was sinless, and there are passages that teach that Muhammad was a man like us (Sura 18:110). Allah even told Muhammad that he must repent of his sins (Sura 40:55). This differs from the Christian teaching that says Jesus Christ lived a perfect and sinless life (2 Corinthians 5:21).

Even though Muslims do not see Muhammad as sinless, they do teach that his life is an example of how they should act. Muhammad's action (known as the *sunna*) provides a clear path for how Muslims are to behave. One Muslim scholar said, "Know that the key to happiness is to follow the sunna and to imitate the Messenger of God in all his coming and going, his movement and rest, in his way of eating, his attitude, his sleep and his talk."[2]

Muhammad's every action is to be imitated by Muslims. His life is considered a model for believers. In fact, some Muslims even avoid eating food that Muhammad avoided or was not able to eat.

Muhammad is so revered by Muslims that no attack upon him or even his likeness (e.g., through a cartoon) is tolerated. William Cantrell Smith notes that "Muslims will allow attacks on Allah: there are atheists and atheistic publications, and rationalistic societies; but to disparage Muhammad will provoke from even the most 'liberal' sections of the community a fanaticism of blazing vehemence."[3]

What do Muslims believe about Jesus?

Muslims sometimes accuse Christians of elevating Jesus to an inappropriate level of honor and worship. The Qur'an teaches that Jesus was just a prophet to the Jews. It also teaches that Jesus promoted the coming of Muhammad, who is revered as the seal of the prophets.

Muhammad originally portrayed himself as the last of the prophets and showed reverence for the People of the Book. So Muslims believe many of the same things about Jesus as Christians do:

- The Qur'an refers to Jesus as "the Messiah" or "the Christ" (Sura 4:157). It also calls Him "the word of God" (Sura 3:45). He is also called a "spirit" from God (Sura 4:171) and a "sign" (Sura 23:50).

- The Qur'an teaches that Jesus was born of the virgin Mary (Sura 19:16-21). It also says that Jesus performed many miracles, including raising people from the dead.

- The Qur'an also claims that Jesus is alive today (Sura 19:33). Many Muslims even believe that He will return to earth.

Though Muslims share some Christian beliefs about Jesus, there are two points of disagreement that mean a world of difference between Islam and Christianity: Christ's death and deity.

Muslims deny that Jesus was crucified on the cross. They base this denial on a passage in the Qur'an that talks about what the Jews did to Jesus:

> That they said (in boast), "We killed Christ Jesus, the Son of Mary, the Messenger of Allah"—but they killed him not, crucified him, but so it was made to appear to them, and those who different therein are full of doubts, with no certain knowledge, but only conjecture to follow, for a surety they killed him not—nay, Allah raised him up to Himself; and Allah is exalted in Power, Wise" (Sura 4:157-158).

Muslims have come to varying conclusions about what this means. Perhaps Judas was mistakenly crucified on the cross. Perhaps a disciple volunteered to die on the cross. Maybe God transposed the likeness of Jesus on some poor soul. There are other suggestions that have been made, but they all point to the same conclusion: Jesus did *not* die on the cross.

Muslims believe that Jesus never died on the cross in part because they cannot believe that a great prophet of God would ever die a shameful death. They believe that God must have intervened so that Jesus would not have to suffer in this way.

They also reject Christ's death on the cross because they reject the Christian idea of original sin and human sinfulness. According to Islam, each person is responsible for his or her actions, and no one else should have to pay for their mistakes. Thus, there was no need for Jesus to die on the cross to atone for our sins. In fact, many Muslims claim that the theology of the atonement was interjected into Christianity at a later date and has corrupted God's original message of salvation.

Muslims also deny Christ's deity. While they respect Him as one of the great prophets, they reject the Christian idea that Jesus was God. They reject the biblical doctrine of the Trinity, and they reinterpret any biblical passage that might suggest that Jesus and God are the same. The Qur'an teaches that it is blasphemy to equate Jesus with God:

> They do blaspheme who say: "Allah is Christ the son of Mary." But said Christ: "O Children of Israel! Worship Allah, my Lord and your Lord." Whoever joins other gods with Allah, Allah will forbid him the Garden, and the Fire will be his abode...Christ, the son of Mary, was no more than a Messenger; many were the Messengers that passed away before him. His mother was a woman of truth. They had both to eat their (daily) food. See how Allah doth make His signs clear to them; yet see in what ways they are deluded away from the truth! (Sura 5:72,75).

The Qur'an also teaches that Christians who "call Christ the Son of God" shall face judgment because "Allah's curse" will be upon them (Sura 9:30).

So it can be said that anyone who accepts the foundational doctrine of Christianity that Jesus is God is guilty of the one unforgivable sin within Islam. Essentially the Qur'an teaches that God will forgive any sin except the sin of idolatry. This means Christians are guilty of the one sin that Allah will not forgive.

By contrast, Christianity teaches that we are saved by believing in Jesus as the Son of God. First John 5:11-12 says, "The testimony is this, that God has given us eternal life, and this life is in His Son. He who has the Son has the life; he who does not have the Son of God does not have the life."

Jesus claimed to be God, Messiah, and the way to God (Mark 14:61-62; John 10:30; 14:6-9). He also allowed others to worship Him (Matthew 14:33; 28:9; see also Acts 10:25-26; 14:12-15). Jesus claimed power over the Sabbath (Matthew 12:8), and He claimed the power to forgive sins (Matthew 9:6; Mark 2:5-10).

What do Muslims believe about the prophets?

The Qur'an teaches that there were many prophets who preceded Muhammad (Sura 2:38,177,252,285; 4:80,164; 17:70; 18:110; 33:40). It mentions 25 prophets by name, although Islamic tradition suggests there were over 100,000 prophets. Muhammad is the "seal" of the prophets (Sura 33:40) and the "bearer of glad tidings" (Sura 33:45-46).

Jesus is mentioned 97 times in the Qur'an. And the Qur'an emphasizes that the messages of Moses and Jesus are the same as the message of Muhammad (Sura 2:136). The Qur'an teaches that prophets were righteous men who brought the word of God. They were free from all vices and thus used by God to deliver His message. Muslims routinely say, "Praise be upon him" after the name of every prophet, including Jesus. Within the Qur'an, Jesus is given high honor, but He is not considered the Son of God.

What do Muslims believe about angels?

According to the Qur'an, angels carry out the commands of Allah (Sura 2:285; 6:100; 34:40-41; 46:29-32; 72:1-28). The most prominent angel in the Qur'an is Gabriel, because he is the one who supposedly appeared to Muhammad and provided Allah's revelation. Michael is another angel mentioned in the Qur'an; he is the guardian of the Jews.

The Qur'an teaches that angels protect us: "We are your protectors in this life and in the hereafter" (Sura 41:31; 82:10-12). The Hadith teaches that two angels are assigned to each person at birth: one records a person's good deeds, the other records a person's bad deeds. They will give an account of each individual's actions on the Day of Judgment.

Islam also teaches that there are jinn. These creatures are said to be invisible and able to act with free will. Like human beings, they have the capacity to be good or bad. They can take various forms and have the capacity to possess humans. Islamic tradition says that Satan was not an angel but a jinn (based upon Islam's understanding of Sura 18:50).

Perhaps the best-known example of a jinn can be found in the story of Aladdin in the Western translation of *The Book of the Thousand and One Nights.* He was bound to an oil lamp and granted wishes to whoever freed him from the lamp by polishing it.

What do Muslims believe about sin?

Islam and Christianity have very different views of sin. Although both accept the Genesis account of creation, they have opposite conclusions about what happened.

The Muslim view is that God created Adam and Eve. They sinned, and God forgave them. Unlike Christianity, Islam does not have a doctrine of original sin. Humans do not have a sin nature, but instead are forgetful of God's commands and therefore need prophets to direct them back to His will.

Allah commanded Muhammad to guide humanity back to the path of salvation through obedience to His laws and the performing of good works. Humans need this guidance because they are described in the Qur'an as ignorant, arrogant, and weak-willed.

Sura 2:35-37 has this account of creation:

> We said, "Oh Adam! Dwell thou and thy wife in the Garden; and eat of the bountiful things therein as (where and when) ye will; but approach not this tree, or ye run into harm and transgression." Then did Satan make them slip from the (Garden), and get them out of the state (of felicity) in what they had been. We said: "Get ye down all (ye people), with enmity between yourselves. On earth will be your dwelling place."…Then learnt Adam from his Lord words of inspiration, and his Lord turned towards him; for He is oft returning, Most Merciful.

This passage and others teach that Adam and Eve disobeyed God, so He expelled them from paradise to earth. In the process, God forgave them. There is no doctrine of the fall, and thus no real need for a Savior to take upon Himself the sins of the world.

One Muslim author wrote,

> Islam teaches that people are born innocent and remain so until each makes him or herself guilty by a guilty deed. Islam does not believe in "original sin"; and its scripture interprets Adam's disobedience as his own personal misdeed—a misdeed for which he repented and which God forgave.[4]

The Christian perspective of sin is very different. Romans 3:23 teaches that "all have sinned and fall short of the glory of God." We are in a fallen state because "through one man sin entered into the world, and death through sin, and so death spread to all men, because all sinned" (Romans 5:12).

What do Muslims believe about salvation?

Islam and Christianity have very different views about salvation that are derived from their different views of sin. Muslims often see human failings as the result of forgetfulness or merely making mistakes. Therefore, Muslims believe people can be saved by their own efforts by following the regimen of the five pillars of Islam: shahadah (repetition of the creed), salat (prayers), zakat (almsgiving), sawm (fast of Ramadan), and hajj (pilgrimage to Mecca).

The Qur'an teaches that believers are to follow the straight path (Sura 1:6). Therefore, they are responsible for their actions. They must do what Allah commands in order to please him and be admitted into paradise. Obeying the five pillars of Islam is the way to achieve this reward.

Muslims do not believe they can have any assurance of their own salvation. Allah sends people to paradise or hell as he pleases: "So Allah leads astray those whom He pleases and guides whom He pleases and He is Exalted in power, full of wisdom" (Sura 14:4).

The Qur'an states that on the Day of Judgment, people's works will be weighed: "Those whose balance (of good deeds) is heavy—they will attain salvation: but those whose balance is light, will be those who have lost their souls; in Hell will they abide" (Sura 23:102-103).

Apparently even Muhammad had doubts about his own salvation. He said, "Though I am the Apostle of Allah, yet I do not know what Allah will do to me" (Hadith 5:266). When Muhammad went on his night journey, he discovered good works recorded in a book:

"The fate of each man. We have bound about his neck. On the Day of Resurrection, We shall confront him with a book spread open, saying 'Here is your book: read it. Enough for you this day that your own soul should call you to account'" (Sura 17:13-14).

The question facing all Muslims is whether their good deeds will outweigh their bad deeds. Faith is certainly important, but so are good works. And because all of this is uncertain, there is no assurance of salvation.

But while salvation is unsure, damnation is certain. The Qur'an teaches that those who reject the faith (Sura 2:6; 3:32) are lost. And a Muslim believer who rejects the teachings of Islam will never be restored. That is why most Muslim parents disown their children if they convert to Christianity. In their minds, Allah has rejected them, so they must do the same.

The biblical view of salvation is very different. The Bible teaches that Adam's sin has affected all humanity. Romans 5:12 reads, "Just as through one man sin entered the world, and death through sin, and so death spread to all men, because all sinned." Paul later adds that

> as through one transgression there resulted condemnation to all men, even so through one act of righteousness there resulted justification of life to all men. For as through the one man's disobedience the many were made sinners, even so through the obedience of the One the many will be made righteous (verses 18-19).

God is holy (Psalm 77:13), and He alone is holy (Revelation 15:4). When we try to measure our sin against God's holiness, it is impossible to balance the scales. David laments in Psalm 130:3 that "if You, LORD, should mark iniquities, O Lord, who could stand?" The Bible also mentions the concept of scales in Daniel 5:27, which mentions God's judgment upon Balshazzar: "You have been weighed on the scales and found deficient." The Bible also uses the image of a measuring rod in Amos 7:7-9 to show that God's people fall short of His standard of righteousness.

The Bible clearly teaches that no one is good enough to stand before God's righteousness. The Old Testament says that "all our righteous deeds are like a filthy garment" (Isaiah 64:6). The New Testament teaches that we are made righteous not by doing good works (Ephesians 2:8-9) but by faith in Christ alone. On the cross, Jesus paid the penalty for sin that we might have everlasting life.

What does the Qur'an teach about the end times?

The Qur'an frequently talks about a coming "Day of Judgment." It is depicted as a time of wrath and retribution (Sura 55). Islam teaches that the final hour will come suddenly, and that natural disasters will occur and graves will open up (Sura 75; 82; 84).

This day is often described as the day of wrath, the day of decision, or the day of truth. On this day, every person will stand before Allah: "On the Day of Judgment We shall bring out for him a scroll, which he will see spread open. It will be said to him, Read thine own record. Sufficient is thy soul this day to make out an account against thee" (Sura 17:13-14).

Also on that day, people's deeds will be weighed on a great scale. If it tips toward righteousness, the person will go to paradise. If not, he or she will go to hell. Allah determines your destiny: "Yea, to Allah belongs all that is in the heavens and on earth; so that He rewards those who do evil, according to their deeds, and He rewards those who do good, with what is best" (Sura 53:31).

According to Islam, paradise is a place of beauty, with streams of clear water as well as rivers of milk and fountains of honey. It is also a place of sensual and sexual delight (Sura 3:14-15; 47:15; 55). And hell is a place of burning. Brains are boiled and molten lead is poured into ears. The poor souls will have faces covered in fire

(Sura 14:50; 76:4). Hell is the place where idolaters and infidels can be found. Also, the Hadith seems to teach that more women are in hell than men.

One Muslim tradition teaches that Jesus will return to earth as the Messiah. Supposedly He will destroy all crosses, kill all pigs, and be buried next to Muhammad when He dies. Another tradition says that a messiah figure (known as *Mahdi*) will come to earth and join with Jesus to fight against the Antichrist. He will then institute a kingdom of justice.

A CHRISTIAN RESPONSE TO ISLAM

CHRISTIANS AND MUSLIMS HAVE a great deal of misunderstanding between them. It is fair to say that Christians often do not understand the basic tenets of Islam, and that Muslims often do not understand the basic theology of biblical Christianity. Moreover, Christians often do not know how to communicate clearly with a Muslim.

This problem has been made worse by the frequent repeating of politically correct phrases that may sound nice but are not true. Statements such as, "Christians and Muslims worship the same God," or "Islam is a religion of peace" frequently cloud the issues and make it more difficult to understand the true nature of Christianity and Islam.

Do Christians and Muslims worship the same God?

One politically correct phrase that is very common but inaccurate is, "Christians and Muslims worship the same God." That might seem to be the case because both Islam and Christianity are monotheistic. But Islam's description of Allah reveals a totally different God than the one worshipped by Christians. Also, Muslims reject the Christian teaching of the Trinity.

Certainly the most foundational doctrine in Islam is that there is only one God. This belief is encapsulated in the creed, "There is no God but Allah, and Muhammad is the prophet of Allah." Not only is this a creed, it is a statement of faith uttered on the lips of every faithful Muslim. It is the creed by which every Muslim is called to prayer five times a day.

Because of this strong emphasis on monotheism, Muslims reject the idea that God could be more than one person or that God could have a partner. The Qur'an teaches that Allah is one God and the same God for all people. Anyone who does not believe this is guilty of the sin of *shirk*. This is the quintessential sin in Islam. According to Islam, God cannot have a partner and cannot be joined together in the Godhead with other persons. Muslims, therefore, reject the Christian idea of the Trinity.

Muslims and Christians also differ in their understanding of the nature and character of God. The God of the Bible is knowable. Jesus came into the world that we might know God (John 17:3).

Islam teaches a very different view of God. Allah is distant, transcendent, and unknowable. He is exalted and far removed from His creation. While we may know His will, we cannot know Him personally. In fact, there is very little written about the character of Allah. He is the creator and sustainer of the creation, but He is also unknowable. No person can ever personally know and have a relationship with Allah. Instead, humans are to be in total submission to the will of Allah.

Moreover, Allah has never personally entered into human history. Instead, he deals with the world through His word (the Qur'an), through His prophets (such as Muhammad), and through angels (such as Gabriel).

By contrast, Christianity teaches the fatherhood of God. Jesus taught in the Lord's Prayer that we may address God as our Father in heaven. Christians can have a personal relationship with God through Christ and call God our Father.

When a Muslim hears a Christian talk about God in such intimate terms, he or she might object. On an emotional level such talk may be appealing. But intellectually, such talk is jarring and considered blasphemous.

Also, the Muslim perspective on God's love is very different. Christians begin with the belief that "God so loved the world" (John 3:16). By contrast, Muslims grow up hearing about all the people Allah does not love: "Allah loves not transgressors" (Sura 2:190); "Allah loves not the unbelievers" (Sura 3:32); and "Allah loves not the evildoers" (Sura 3:57).

Why do Muslims reject the idea that Jesus is the Son of God?

As we have mentioned, the Qur'an refers to Jesus as "the Messiah" or "the Christ" (Sura 4:157) and also calls Him "the word of God" (Sura 3:45). But Muslims reject the idea that Jesus is the Son of God.

Sura 19:35 says, "It is not befitting Allah that He should beget a son. Glory to Him! When He determines a matter, He only says to it, 'Be,' and it is." Muhammad believed that for Allah to beget a son would essentially make Allah a sexual animal, so he rejected the idea that God could have a Son. He believed that it would be beneath God's dignity to have sexual relations. Sura 2:116 says, "They say, 'Allah hath begotten a son': Glory be to Him—Nay, to Him belongs all that is in the heavens and on earth: everything renders worship to Him."

Some Muslim commentators have said that the idea that God could have a son is a relic of paganism. They even believe that it is blasphemous to say that "Allah begets sons like a man or animal."[1]

This, however, is not what Christianity teaches. The Bible does not say that God had sex and begat a son. While Greek mythology spoke of gods who had sex with each other and with humans, Christianity teaches no such thing about God.

The Bible specifically calls Jesus Christ the Son of God. God the Father Himself declared from heaven, "This is My beloved Son, with whom I am well-pleased" (Matthew 17:5). Also, believers are called children of God: "See how great a love the Father has bestowed on us, that we would be called children of God" (1 John 3:1).

How should Christians respond to Islam's rejection of the Trinity?

Islam was founded in order to return all religions to a true worship of the one true God. Muslims, therefore, reject any religion that is not monotheistic. The doctrine of the Trinity, to Muslims, sounds like a corruption of monotheism. It seems contrary to teachings about the unity and oneness of God.

Two key verses in the Qur'an comment on the doctrine of the Trinity. One is Sura 4:171, which says, "O people of the book! Commit no excesses in your religions: nor say of Allah aught but the truth. Christ Jesus the son of Mary was (no more than) a messenger of Allah, and His World, which He bestowed on Mary." The verse continues, "Say not 'Trinity': desist: it will be better for you; for Allah is One God: glory be to Him."

The other passage is Sura 5:73: "They do blaspheme who say: 'Allah is one of three in a Trinity' for there is no God except One God. If they desist not from their word (of blasphemy), verily, a grievous penalty will befall the blasphemers among them."

Later in Sura 5 there is a conversation that supposedly takes place between Jesus and God on judgment day:

> And behold! Allah will say: "O Jesus the son of Mary! Didst thou say unto men, 'Worship me and my mother as gods in derogation of Allah?'" He will say, "Glory to

> Thee! Never could I say what I had no right (to say). Had
> I said such a thing, Thou wouldst indeed have known it.
> Thou knowest what is in my heart, though I know not
> what is in Thine....Never said I to them aught except
> what Thou didst command me to say, to wit, 'Worship
> Allah—my Lord and your Lord.'"

The Bible clearly states that there is only one God. Deuteronomy 6:4 states, "Hear O Israel, the Lord is our God, the Lord is one." Isaiah 44:6 states, "I am the first and I am the last, and there is no God besides me." Clearly, these verses reveal that there is only one God. Yet the Bible also teaches God has revealed Himself in three distinct persons. There are three separate persons in the Bible who are called God and have the characteristics only God can have. They are the Father, the Son, and the Holy Spirit. These three persons make up the one true God. These three persons are of the same substance, equal in power and glory.

Throughout Scripture, the Father is called God. The Son is also called God (Matthew 1:23; John 20:28; Titus 2:13). The Son is worshipped and has authority over things only God has authority over. The Son also shares in the attributes only God can have. The Holy Spirit is also called God (Matthew 28:19; Acts 5:3-4; Romans 8). All three are equal in nature yet there is an economy among the persons of the Trinity.

We also see that the disciples referred to Jesus as God. Thomas, after seeing the resurrected Lord, proclaims to Jesus, "My Lord and My God!" (John 20:28). And when John wrote his Gospel, he began by saying, "In the beginning was the Word, and the Word was with God, and the Word was God" (John 1:1).

Isn't Muhammad like every other founder of a religion?

One statement often heard in religion classes on college campuses is that "Muhammad is like every other founder of a religion."

This simply is not the case. For example, nearly every major religion in the world teaches a variation of the Golden Rule: "Do unto others as you would have them do unto you."

Islam does not have any teaching that is comparable to the Golden Rule. Instead, it makes very definite distinctions in the way Muslims are to treat believers and unbelievers. The latter are called infidels and are often treated harshly or killed. In this way, Islam is very different from other religions.

Let's compare Jesus and Muhammad. Muslims believe that Muhammad is the final prophet from Allah. He is referred to as the "seal of the prophets" (Sura 33:40). But while he is revered as the greatest of the prophets, most do not teach that he was sinless. The Qur'an does not make the claim that he was sinless, and there are passages that teach Muhammad was a man like the rest of us (Sura 18:110). In addition, Allah told Muhammad that he must repent of his sins (Sura 40:55).

By contrast, Jesus claimed to be God and claimed to have powers and authority that only God could possess. The New Testament provides eyewitness accounts that affirm Jesus' claims and miracles. Moreover, 2 Corinthians 5:21 tells us Jesus lived a perfect and sinless life.

Muhammad taught that Muslims are to fight on behalf of Allah (Sura 4:76) and fight against unbelievers (Sura 9:123). By contrast, Jesus taught that Christians are to love their enemies (Matthew 5:44) and turn the other cheek (Matthew 5:39).

So, Muhammad was different from many others who founded a religion. And Muhammad was very different from Jesus Christ.

How do Muslims view the Christian world?

Most Muslims in other parts of the world have a great misunderstanding of Western Christianity. Often their experiences with the United States and the rest of the world are limited to one of our cultural exports: the media. What they know about us is defined by our movies, music, and television programs. Thus, they perceive America and the rest of the Western world as full of sex and violence. Because they believe that America is a Christian nation, they assume that everything that comes from our country (and the rest of the West) represents Christian attitudes and behavior. So they often equate Christianity with promiscuous sex, rampant drug use, violence, and social strife.

When you talk with a Muslim, you should clarify that what he or she sees in Western society frequently does not necessarily align with biblical Christianity. Christians are equally concerned about the sex, pornography, violence, and profanity in the media and in real life. Help your Muslim acquaintance to understand that Christians have concerns about these very same issues.

Why is it hard for Muslims to become Christians?

One reason it is hard for Muslims to be drawn to Christianity is they equate Western decadence with Christianity. They reason: If that's what Christianity is, then I don't want any part of it. It is important to clear up many of the misconceptions Muslims may have about Christianity.

Culture is another reason it is hard for Muslims to become Christians. It has been said that Islam is 10 percent theological and 90 percent cultural. To reject Islam is to reject one's family and culture. The average Muslim desires (as we all do) to be part of a larger cultural group that provides us with security and affirmation.

The Muslim culture also reinforces these beliefs and provides a safe haven in a world full of danger and confusion. When a Muslim hears the claims of Christ, he or she may be drawn to the truth but refuse to make a commitment because of the heavy cost of doing so. Leaving Islam can mean the loss of family, the loss of community, even the loss of life.

A Muslim needs to be able to find a safe Christian community to join after his or her conversion. Unfortunately, in many parts of the world, such communities do not exist.

How can we witness to Muslims about Jesus?

Muslims accept that the Qur'an teaches them all they need to know about Jesus Christ. They accept that He is the Messiah and the Christ. And they honor Him as one of the greatest prophets. So they feel they already believe everything that needs to be believed about Him. That's why they feel uncomfortable when Christians tell them that they need to put their faith in Jesus Christ. After all, they *already* believe in Him and *already* honor Him.

While Muslims may know that the Qur'an calls Jesus "Messiah" and the "word of God," they have no context for understanding what those titles mean. You can explain what these titles meant in the Old Testament and how they found their fulfillment in the person of Jesus Christ.

Show them from the Qur'an what it really says about Jesus. For example, Sura 3:42-55 teaches that (1) Mary was chosen by God, (2) Jesus was born of a virgin, (3) Jesus is the Messiah, (4) Jesus has power over death, and (5) Jesus knows the way to heaven. These verses ascribe power and position to Jesus that Muhammad did not ascribe to himself.

Many Muslims are not aware that the following assertions appear in the Qur'an:

- If you are in doubt about the truth, ask those who read the Scripture that came before you (Sura 10:94).

- To be a proper Muslim, one must read the Old and New Testament, known as the Before Books (Sura 4:136).

- Those who observe the teaching of the Torah and the Gospels will go to heaven (Sura 5:65-66).

- Mohammed states he is not the greatest prophet, he does not know what will happen to his followers (after death), and he only came to warn the people about the fate (Sura 46:9).

These passages are great conversation-starters about the Bible, Jesus, and salvation. They give Muslims permission to read the Bible and to learn spiritual truth from Christians.

Finally, make sure you talk about the love of God. As we have mentioned, Muslims believe that Allah is distant and unknowable. Christianity offers to them the possibility of knowing God personally. This is attractive to Muslims.

A seminary conducted a survey of 600 former Muslims who had become Christians. One of the most significant factors involved in their conversions was an emphasis on the love of God and the intimacy that believers can enjoy with God as their heavenly Father.[2] In light of this information, it's important to talk about the love of God when sharing your faith with a Muslim.[3]

MISCONCEPTIONS ABOUT ISLAM

THOUGH ISLAM IS THE SECOND LARGEST religion in the world, many Christians do not know even the most basic tenets of this faith. And any misunderstandings we might have about Islam are likely to be worsened by all sorts of politically correct statements that misrepresent the truth about Islam. Politicians, religious leaders, and the media spread many misperceptions about Islam that are simply not true and do a disservice to our understanding of this religion. Let's look now at some of these misperceptions.

Is Islam a religion of peace?

One politically correct phrase we hear often is that "Islam is a religion of peace." While it is true that many Muslims are peace-loving, is it also true that Islam is a religion of peace? To answer that question, it is important to understand the meaning of the word *jihad.*

Although some Muslims understand jihad to be merely intellectual and philosophical, the usual translation of jihad involves a holy war. That has been the traditional interpretation since the time of Muhammad.

Spencer: "When you come to chapter nine (which is the last chapter of the Qur'an chronologically), you get these verses that enjoin warfare against unbelievers and single out the people of the book (Jews and Christians primarily) as being the people that Muslims must war against. This is, according to the great Qur'anic commentator, Ibn Kathir (and others whose works are still influential in the Islamic world), the Qur'an's last word on jihad and the last word on the relationships to Muslims to non-Muslims. Ibn Kathir, in his commentary on the Qur'an (which is the mainstream and widely read commentary today) says that the ninth chapter, and particularly the verse of the sword (Sura 9:5), which says, 'Slay the unbelievers wherever you find them,' abrogates every peace treaty in the Qur'an and leaves war its last word. And on this basis, Muslims have waged war for centuries since then."

—Interview with Robert Spencer on *Point of View* radio talk show[1]

Jihad is to be waged on the battlefield. Sura 47:4 says, "When you meet the unbelievers in the battlefield, strike off their heads and, when you have laid them low, bind your captives firmly." Sura 9:5 says, "Fight and slay the pagans wherever you find them, and seize them, beleager them, and lie in wait for them in every stratagem." Consider some additional Qur'anic passages concerning jihad:

- "Fight in the cause of Allah those who fight you…and slay them wherever you catch them…and fight them on until there is no more tumult or oppression, and there prevail justice and faith in Allah" (Sura 2:190-193).

- "Soon shall We cast terror into the hearts of the unbelievers, for that they joined companions with Allah, for what He had no authority: their abode will be the Fire: And evil is the home of the wrong-doers" (Sura 3:151).

- "O ye who believe! Fight the unbelievers who gird you about, and let them find firmness in you; and know that Allah is with those who fear Him" (Sura 9:123).

Muslims are also to wage jihad not only against unbelievers but against those who have strayed from the faith:

- "They but wish that ye should reject Faith, as they do, and thus be on the same footing (as they): so take not friends from their ranks until they flee in the way of Allah...But if they turn renegades, seize them and slay them wherever ye find them" (Sura 4:89).

- "Prophet, make war on the unbelievers and the hypocrites and deal rigorously with them. Hell shall be their home: and evil fate" (Sura 9:73).

The Qur'an also teaches that engaging in jihad is good for a Muslim: "Fighting is prescribed upon you, and ye dislike it. But it is possible that ye dislike a thing which is good for you, and that ye love a thing which is bad for you. But Allah knoweth and ye know not" (Sura 2:216). The Qur'an also exalts "those who strive and fight in the cause of Allah with their goods and persons" above "those who sit and receive no hurt" (4:95).

Another way to understand the term *jihad* is to look at the historical context in which the term has been used. After Muhammad's success in the Battle of Badr, he set forth various principles of warfare. For example, according to Sura 9:29, jihad is a religious duty. Muhammad taught (in Sura 3:157-158,195; 9:111) that martyrdom in jihad is the highest good and guarantees salvation. Sura 9:5 says that Muslims engaged in jihad should not show tolerance toward unbelievers. And acts of terrorism are justified in Sura 8:2.

Muhammad also promised that followers would be victorious in jihad even when they were outnumbered. "Exhort the believers to fight. If there be of you twenty steadfast they shall overcome two hundred, and if there be of you a hundred (steadfast) they shall overcome a thousand of those who disbelieve, because they (the disbelievers) are a folk without intelligence" (Sura 8:65).

In a recent survey on global conflict, Monty Marshall and Ted Burr of the Center for International Development and Conflict Management found that of the 24 major armed conflicts taking place worldwide in 2005, more than half (13) involved Muslim governments or paramilitary groups on one or both sides of the fighting. What's more, among six countries with "emerging armed conflicts," four are predominantly Muslim and another, Thailand, involves a Muslim separatist movement.

Marshall and Burr also rated 161 countries according to their capacity to avoid outbreaks of armed conflicts. Whereas 63 percent of non-Muslim countries were categorized as "enjoy[ing] the strongest prospects for successful management of new challenges," just 18 percent of the 50 Muslim nations included were similarly designated. In addition, Muslim nations (those with at least 40 percent of the population being Muslim) were two-and-a-half times more likely than non-Muslim nations to be considered "at the greatest risk of neglecting or mismanaging emerging societal crises such that these conflicts escalate to serious violence and/or government instability."[2]

Some of the violence commanded in the Qur'an is actually quite gruesome:

- "The punishment of those who wage war against Allah and His Messenger, and strive with might and main for mischief through the land is: execution, or crucifixion, or the cutting off of hands and feet from opposite sides, or exile from the land: that is their disgrace in this world, and a punishment is theirs in the hereafter" (Sura 5:33).

- "Smite ye above their necks and smite all their fingertips off them. This because they contend against Allah and His Messenger, Allah is strict in punishment" (Sura 8:12-13).

Doesn't the Qur'an prohibit murder?

In defense of Islam, Muslims sometimes quote a passage in the Qur'an to show that it prohibits murder: "Whosoever kills a human being for other than manslaughter or corruption in the earth, it shall be as if he had killed all mankind, and whoever saves the life of one, it shall be as if he had saved the life of all mankind" (Sura 5:32).

This passage is not really a prohibition against murder, for two reasons. First, the passage (Sura 5:32) begins with the address to the "Children of Israel." This represents a particular historical context. It is not addressed to Muslims. Rather, it is a warning to the Jews not to engage in warfare against Muhammad.

Second, it has an important proviso: if there is "corruption in the earth." This is sometimes translated as "making mischief in the land." While this would certainly include making war against the Muslims, it could also include resisting the Muslim advance into the land. The penalty for making mischief in the land was "execution, or crucifixion, or the cutting off of hands and feet from opposite sides, or exile from the land."

Isn't the Bible just as violent as the Qur'an?

Whenever verses of the sword from the Qur'an are quoted, usually someone will point out that the Old Testament of the Bible also calls for violence. But are the Qur'an and the Bible morally equivalent? Let's compare some passages and see.

The Qur'an calls for jihad against the unbelievers (or infidels). Sura 9:5 says, "Fight and slay the pagans wherever you find them, and seize them, beleager them, and lie in wait for them in every stratagem."

Sura 9:29 says

> Fight those who believe not in Allah nor the Last Day, nor hold that forbidden which hath been forbidden by Allah and His Prophet, nor acknowledge the religion of Truth, (even if they are) of the People of the Book, until they pay the *jizyah* [per capita tax imposed on non-Muslim adult males] with willing submission, and feel themselves subdued.

Sura 47:4-7 says

> When you meet unbelievers, smite their necks, then, when you have made wide slaughter among them, tie fast the bonds; then set them free, either by grace or ransom, till the war lays down its loads…And those who are slain in the way of God, He will not send their works astray. He will guide them, and dispose their minds aright, and He will admit them to Paradise, that He has made known to them.

Note that the calls for jihad that appear in the Qur'an are very general—the verses apply against all non-Muslims at all times. By contrast, the Old Testament's calls for military action are always against specific groups at specific times. For example, Deuteronomy 7:1-2 says,

> When the LORD your God brings you into the land where you are entering to possess it, and clears away many nations

before you, the Hittites and the Girgashites and the Amor-
ites and the Canaanites and the Perizzites and the Hivites
and the Jebusites, seven nations greater and stronger than
you, and when the LORD your God delivers them before
you and you defeat them, then you shall utterly destroy
them. You shall make no covenant with them and show
no favor to them.

In 1 Samuel 15:2-3 we read,

Thus says the LORD of hosts, "I will punish Amalek for
what he did to Israel, how he set himself against him on
the way while he was coming up from Egypt. Now go
and strike Amalek and utterly destroy all that he has, and
do not spare him; but put to death both man and woman,
child and infant, ox and sheep, camel and donkey."

Again, notice that in the Old Testament, these were *direct* and
specific commands to fight against a particular group of people.
These passages do not apply to anyone who is not a Hittite,
Girgashite, Amorite, Canaanite, Perizzite, Hivite, Jebusite, or Ama-
lekite. These commands given during the Old Testament theocracy
of Israel applied only to those people at that time.

In 1 Samuel 15, the military action was to be taken only against
the Amalekites. In fact, in verse 6, Israel's King Saul said to the
Kenites, "Go, depart, go down from among the Amalekites, so that
I do not destroy you with them." So specific is the command that
Saul sent the Kenites away so they might not be hurt or become
collateral damage in the battle against the Amalekites.

While the calls to military action in the Old Testament apply
to particular groups of people, the calls for jihad in the Qur'an
apply to all unbelievers at all times. The commands are universally
binding to all Muslims at all times.

No Christian leader today is calling for a holy war against infidels. But many Muslim leaders cite the Qur'an for that very action. Osama bin Laden, for example, has quoted verses of the sword within his various fatwas (decrees).

Contrast this with the New Testament, which calls for Christians to love their enemies (Matthew 5:44) and turn the other cheek (Matthew 5:39). Christians are called to love and not hate their enemies, to pray for them, and to not respond with violence against those with whom they disagree.

"There was a brilliant but paranoid Egyptian writer by the name of Sayyid Qutb, imprisoned in Egypt in 1956. In 1970, he published a book, *In the Shade of the Koran,* attacking the West as totally corrupt. Qutb knew what he was talking about. He lived in the U.S. for a time and saw our decadence. He also read Western philosophers like [Martin] Heidegger and [Jacques] Derrida and other intellectuals who hated the West. And he read all the anti-Zionist, anti-Semitic literature.

"Qutb's *In the Shade of the Koran* unequivocally advocates killing of 'infidels.' He was executed by the Egyptian government, but his brother, Muhammad Qutb, escaped Egypt, went to Saudi Arabia, and became a professor at the university. One of his star pupils: none other than Osama bin Laden. Don't tell me worldviews don't matter. This same worldview now influences millions of radical Muslims—up to 10 percent, according to some accounts, 100 million. What we're seeing in the Middle East today aren't isolated acts of terrorism, but a widespread, well-organized, hatred-fueled movement."[3]

—Charles Colson

Did dancing in an American church fuel Muslim anger?

Back in 1948, Sayyid Qutb visited the United States for Egypt's Ministry of Education. His experience in America influenced his perception of the West. He saw many examples of what he perceived as moral degeneracy and sexual promiscuity.

Sayyid Qutb wrote that even American religion was tainted by materialism and consumerism. He felt that churches used Madison Avenue marketing techniques to promote their services. The churches, he felt, were like merchants and entertainers. Success, big numbers, and having a good time seemed to be foundational to American churches.[4]

Qutb was especially shocked by the clergy-sanctioned dances at church recreation halls. When the lights were lowered, the dancing became hot. Here is his description of what he saw: "The dance is inflamed by the notes of the gramophone…the dance-hall becomes a whirl of heels and thighs, arms enfold hips, lips and breasts meet, and the air is full of lust."[5]

Because Sayyid Qutb was dark-skinned, he also experienced racism in the United States. By the time he returned to Egypt, he joined the Muslim Brotherhood organization.[6] Imprisonment and torture while in Egypt made his writings more militant, and he ultimately became an architect of radical Islam. A militant offshoot of the Muslim Brotherhood is Islamic Jihad, whose members assassinated Egyptian president Anwar Sadat. Osama bin Laden is among those who have been influenced by the Muslim Brotherhood.

Bernard Lewis says that Sayyid Qutb's denunciations of America's moral decadence have been incorporated into radical Islamic theology. For example, Iran's Ayatollah Khomeini called the United States the Great Satan. He was being consistent with the Qur'an's depictions of Satan as a seducer and "the insidious tempter who whispers in the hearts of men."[7]

What is the significance of the Muslim names for weapons?

Even the names Muslims have assigned to rockets and missiles have jihadic significance. For example, consider the Khaibar-1 rockets that Hezbollah launched into Israel. During these attacks, demonstrators chanted: "Khaybar, Khaybar, O Jews, the army of Muhammad will return." A leading Muslim cleric in Lebanon spoke of a "new battle of Khaybar." What does *Khaybar* mean?

The mainstream press didn't do a very good job of explaining this term. The Associated Press said that *Khaybar* is the name of an oasis in Saudi Arabia. But if you know the history of Islam, the term takes on more significance. Khaybar is a place where Muhammad won a pivotal battle against some Jews in the year A.D. 629. Muhammad and his forces attacked without provocation.

One Muslim observer remembered:

> We met the workers of Khaybar coming out in the morning with their spades and baskets. When they saw the apostle and the army, they cried, "Muhammad with his force," and turned tail and fled. The apostle said, "Allah Akbar! Khaybar is destroyed. When we arrive in a people's square it is a bad morning for those who have been warned."[8]

Muhammad's earliest biographer wrote, "The apostle seized the forts one by one as he came to them" and another biographer reported that Muhammad "killed ninety-three men of the Jews."

In an effort to locate the Jews' wealth, Muhammad had one man tortured and eventually killed. He later married the man's wife as a war prize. Although some Jews were allowed to live and go into exile, Muhammad later killed others and enslaved the women of the tribe.

When the name *Khaybar* is invoked today, it has more meaning than many Westerners might imagine. Those involved in jihad warfare are recalling an aggressive raid by Muhammad that resulted in the eradication of Jews from the Arabian Peninsula. In giving this name to their rockets and missiles, they are calling for the same actions today.

ISLAM AND HUMAN RIGHTS

CHRISTIANS IN THE WESTERN WORLD accept the concept of a true separation of the institutions of church and state. Hundreds of years of Western tradition have demonstrated the wisdom of maintaining this separation and the danger that ensues when the ecclesiastical and civil institutions are melded into one.

Bernard Lewis, Professor Emeritus of Near Eastern Studies at Princeton University, explains that no such separation exists in Islam:

> In [the Islamic] world, religion embraces far more than it does in the Christian or post-Christian world. We are accustomed to talking of church and state and a whole series of pairs of words that go with them—lay and ecclesiastical, secular and religious, spiritual and temporal, and so on. These pairs of words simply do not exist in classical Islamic terminology because the dichotomy that these words express is unknown.[1]

Because such words and their equivalent concepts do not exist in Islam, it is difficult to see how to form democracies in the Muslim world. Essential to the functioning of democracies is a belief in the separation of powers. This would include not only a horizontal separation of powers (executive, legislative, and judicial), but a religious separation of powers (ecclesiastical and civil). Islam knows no such separations.

What is sharia law?

A foundational practice of Islam is the implementation of sharia into the legal structure. The term *sharia* is derived from the verb *shara'a,* which is a system of divine law, belief, or practice that shapes all of life. It applies to economics, politics, and society. Most Muslims distinguish between *fiqh* (which deals with the details of Islam) and *sharia* (which refers to the principles behind those details). Ideally, both should be in harmony with each other.

Sometimes the world has been able to see how extreme the interpretation of sharia can be. For example, when the Taliban ruled in Afghanistan, a woman was accused of adultery because she was found in the company of a man who was not a close family member. She was stoned to death.[2] In another case, a woman and a man accused of adultery were stoned to death in a public assembly using palm-sized stones.[3] Other extreme examples of sharia law have surfaced in countries such as Sudan and Nigeria.

Are Jews and Christians second-class citizens?

The Qur'an talks about "the People of the Book," or Christians and Jews. Sura 9:29 says,

> Fight those who believe not in Allah nor the Last Day, nor hold that forbidden which hath been forbidden by Allah and His Prophet, nor acknowledge the religion of Truth, (even if they are) of the People of the Book, until they pay the jizyah with willing submission, and feel themselves subdued.

Islamic law refers to "the People of the Book," or Christians and Jews, as *dhimmis*. In Muslim countries, they have protected status and can live as "protected people" (*Ahl al-dhimma*). But they have to live as second-class citizens in a Muslim state.

Muhammad made a distinction between infidels, or pagans and polytheists, and "the People of the Book," who had received revelations from prophets such as Moses and Jesus. The latter group is "protected" in a sense because they had received these revelations. But Christians and Jews are also guilty because, according to Islam, they have distorted these teachings and rejected the teachings of Muhammad. Although this status was originally given only to Christians and Jews, it was later extended to other religions (Sikhs, Zoroastrians, etc.).

Islamic teaching stipulates that Jews and Christians may live in a Muslim country, but not as equals to other Muslims. Usually this means they may not participate in the government. They may practice their religion, but with many restrictions. In the past, and sometimes today, this meant they were not allowed to exhibit any external manifestations of worship (a procession with the cross, the ringing of bells).

These restrictions are another part of Sura 9:29, which requires dhimmis to "feel themselves subdued." In the past this has meant: (1) they could not prevent a fellow Christian from converting to Islam, (2) they could not erect a cross on their church building, and (3) they must dress in a way that identifies them as Jews or Christians.

Finally, dhimmis must pay the *jizya,* a poll tax. In earlier times, this was a major source of income for the Muslim government.

The Qur'an teaches that "there is no compulsion in religion" (2:256). But is that really so? It depends upon your definition of compulsion. A closer look at Islamic law demonstrates a veiled threat that many believe is tantamount to compulsion. For example,

Muhammad instructed his followers to invite non-Muslims to accept Islam before waging war against them. If they refused, warfare would follow, or second-class status. The non-Muslims would be inferiors in the Muslim social order and pay the jizya as required by Sura 9:29. If they pay it, they may live, but if they refuse to pay it, warfare will ensue.

How have Christians been treated within Islam?

After its rapid expansion in the seventh century, Islam developed a practice of allowing Jews and Christians to live within Muslim society but with many restrictions. The Pact of Umar set forth 28 limitations on their rights and practices.[4] For example, Christians:

- "shall not build, in our cities or in their neighborhood, new monasteries, churches, convents, or monks' cells, nor shall we repair, by day or by night, such of them as fall in ruins or are situated in the quarters of the Muslims"

- "shall not manifest our religion publicly nor convert anyone to it"

- "shall not prevent any of our kin from entering Islam if they wish it"

- "shall not display our crosses or our books in the roads or markets of the Muslims" and "shall only use clappers in our churches very softly"

- "shall not raise our voices in our church services or in the presence of Muslims nor shall we raise our voices when following our dead"

Today, the application of "dimmitude" varies from country to country. In many Muslim countries, non-Muslims must pay the jizya and must wear a wide cloth belt, known as the *zunnar*, to identify them. Sometimes they must keep to the side of the street. And they are never greeted with the traditional Muslim greeting, "As-Salamu 'alaykum" (which means "Peace be with you").[5]

In many cases, non-Muslims are persecuted and killed. A number of excellent books document the ways in which Christians have been persecuted in Muslim countries.[6] For example, from 1905 to 1918, over two million Armenian Christians were slaughtered by the Ottoman Turks. Since Muslims came to power in Sudan and declared jihad on Christians, there have been more than three million Christians killed.

What happens to those who leave Islam and are considered apostate?

It is difficult for a Muslim to leave the Islamic faith. A Muslim is considered part of a larger community of Muslim believers. He or she is a member of the *umma*, which is an Arabic word meaning "community" or "nation."

When a Muslim decides to leave the faith, there are repercussions in both the family and the community. The family is embarrassed and will lose respect within the Muslim community. The mosque feels it has failed in its duty and lost a member to ignorance and idolatry.

The Qur'an teaches that an apostate Muslim faces the wrath of Allah (Sura 47:25-28). Sharia law in many countries treats apostasy as the unforgivable sin; therefore, it is punishable by death. Often those who depart are referred to as *kafir*, which, in Arabic, means "unbeliever." This word is used to speak of those who reject the teachings of Islam and the Qur'an.

Many Muslim countries have laws against apostasy. Islam teaches that once you are a Muslim, you are always a Muslim. Leaving the Muslim faith can have harsh consequences, including death.

Point of View: "The Qu'ran, in Sura 48:29, says, 'Mohammed is the apostle of Allah, those who follow him are merciful to one another but ruthless to unbelievers.' But you have pointed out how radical Islam does not believe in equality, dignity, and the rights of people. You have to go no further than looking at the abuse of women under radical Islamic groups to see that they do not believe in human rights."

Spencer: "As a matter of fact, Islamic groups themselves have made no secret of this. After the Universal Declaration of Human Rights was issued by the United Nations in 1948, the Organization of Islamic Conference [56 Islamic states in the world] came together and issued an Islamic Declaration of Human Rights which emphasized that there could be no granting of any idea of human rights that contradicted Islamic law. This [declaration] rules out freedom of conscience and equality of rights for women and equality of rights for non-Muslims in Islamic society."

—Interview with **Robert Spencer** on *Point of View* radio talk show[7]

What does the Qur'an teach about women?

There is great confusion about the status of women within Islam. Some Muslim leaders claim that Islam actually liberates women. One Muslim women's advocate said that the "Islamic religion has given women more rights than any other religion has, and has guaranteed her honour and pride."[8] That might surprise the women who lived under the Taliban in Afghanistan, or who live under sharia law in many Muslims countries today.

While it is true that many Muslims no doubt do respect and honor women, it is not true that such attitudes can be found in the Qur'an. Here are just a few passages that describe the way women are to be treated:

1. According to the Qur'an women are considered inferior to men: "Men have authority over women because God has made the one superior to the other" (Sura 4:34).

2. The Qur'an restricts a woman's testimony in court. Her testimony is worth half as much as that of a man (Sura 2:282).

3. The Qur'an teaches that a son's inheritance should be twice that of a daughter's: "Allah thus directs you as regards your children's inheritance; to the male, a portion equal to that of two females" (Sura 4:11).

4. Islam sanctions polygamy (up to four wives) as well as sex with slave women: "If we fear that ye shall not be able to deal justly with the orphans, marry women of your choice, two or three or four; but if we fear that ye shall not be able to deal justly with them, then only one, or a captive that your hand possess, that will be more suitable, to prevent you from doing injustice" (Sura 4:3)

5. If wives are disloyal or disobedient to their husbands, the Qur'an sets forth the following punishment: The husband is first to admonish her, then not sleep with her, and then to beat her lightly. Essentially, wives are subject to the control of their husbands (Sura 2:223; 4:34).

What does the Qur'an teach about polygamy?

In Arabia before the time of Muhammad, polygamy was common. A man could have as many wives as he could support. The Qur'an permitted a man to have two, three, or four wives. Muhammad himself claimed to have had a special revelation that allowed him to have more than four wives. The Qur'an also taught that he could marry prisoners of war, daughters of uncles and aunts, and any believing woman (Sura 33:50).

Even though the Qur'an permits polygamy, many Islamic nations today prohibit multiple wives. Turkey, for example, banned polygamy in 1926. Also, Islamic law allows a Muslim man to marry a non-Muslim woman, but a Muslim woman cannot marry a non-Muslim man.

There is also the Islamic concept of Mut'a, which allows a Muslim man to take a temporary "wife" for a sexual relationship. This may be done when he is in military service, although some have abused this "privilege" to justify taking a prostitute as a temporary "wife" for a night.

How do Muslim women participate in worship?

Sometimes women participate in public prayer in mosques, other times they do not. A formal prayer in a mosque is a public demonstration of a Muslim's faith. But women's participation varies according to culture and time period. At the times that women do attend, they are segregated from the men and wear their veils.

Why do Muslim women wear veils and scarves?

The veiling and seclusion of women has been a part of Muslim culture since the beginnings of Islam. In the Qur'an, Muhammad commanded his wives and daughters to draw veils around them, and this command has been applied to all Muslim women. The veil would allow them to be recognized but not molested (Sura 33:59).

The Qur'an teaches that women must

> lower their gaze and guard their modesty: that they should not display their beauty and ornaments except what must ordinarily appear thereof: that they should draw their veils

over their bosoms and not display their beauty except to
their husbands, their fathers (Sura 24:31).

The veils do more than just cover the face and body of women;
they establish the significant distinction between men and women
and separate women from men and from public life.

Women cover themselves in different ways in different Muslim
cultures, ranging from burkas to scarves. Sometimes the command
for women to cover themselves has had tragic consequences. In
March 2002, 15 girls died in a school fire in Saudi Arabia. Because
there were no men in the school, the girls were permitted to remove
their Islamic garb in class. When the fire broke out in the building,
they tried to escape but were stopped by the Saudi religious police
(known as the muttawa), who would not allow the girls to leave
the building because they were not veiled. The police apparently
reasoned that death for the girls was preferable to the risk of sub-
jecting men in the vicinity to impure thoughts.

"There's a new fashion on college campuses, but it's not one
you'll find at Abercrombie any time soon. It's the *higab,* the
traditional Muslim headscarf that denotes modesty and reverence to God, and it's being worn by increasing numbers of
young Muslim American women. By most accounts, they are
the American-born children of the estimated 4 million Muslims
who immigrated to the United States over the last 40 years.
The irony: many of those parents abandoned their Islamic
cultural identities to assimilate into American society...Spurred
by a desire to express solidarity in the face of post-9/11 discrimination, young Muslim Americans are connecting with their
Islamic heritage and embracing a religious culture many of
them had known only secondhand."[9]

—**Matthew Phillips,** *in Newsweek*

Why can't women go out alone in Muslim countries?

Islamic law states that a "husband may forbid his wife to leave the home."[10] It also states that "a woman may not leave the city without her husband or a member of her unmarriageable kin accompanying her, unless the journey is obligatory, like the hajj. It is unlawful for her to travel otherwise, and unlawful for her husband to allow her to."[11]

These laws were practiced in Afghanistan under the Taliban, and are observed in countries such as Saudi Arabia. There, women cannot drive nor can they leave their home without being accompanied by a male family member. Amnesty International reports that women in Saudi Arabia "who walk unaccompanied, or are in the company of a man who is neither their husband nor close relative, are at risk of arrest on suspicion of prostitution" or other moral offenses.[12]

What does Islam teach about divorce?

Divorce is very easy to carry out under Islam. All a husband needs to do is say to his wife, "I divorce you." The divorce is final at that moment. The Qur'an does, however, provide a mechanism for resolving disputes: "If a wife fears cruelty or desertion on her husband's part, there is no blame on them if they arrange an amicable settlement between themselves; and such settlements is best" (Sura 4:128).

The Qur'an also instructs men to observe a waiting period to make sure their divorced wife is not pregnant: "if you divorce your wives, divorce them at the end of their waiting period" (Sura 65:1). In reality, however, a woman can be divorced and put out of the house in minutes.

Sura 65 also seems to provide justification for child marriage. Following the verse about divorce, we read, "The same shall apply to those who have not yet menstruated" (Sura 65:4). This passage seems to consider the possibility that a man may be married to a girl who has not even reached adolescence.

Child marriages were common in the Arabian Peninsula during the time that the Qur'an was written. One of Muhammad's wives was a child bride of six, and he apparently consummated the marriage when she was nine years old.

Such marriages are still common in some Muslim countries today. It is estimated that half the teenage girls in some countries (such as Afghanistan) are already married.[13] Iranian girls can get married with parental permission when they are as young as nine, or 13 without parental consent.[14]

What is the Muslim law concerning rape?

We have already noted that a woman's testimony in a court of law is equal to half of a man's testimony. When it comes to an accusation of rape, there must be four adult males of "impeccable" character who can confirm the woman's accusation. In fact, they must see the act itself (e.g., witness the penetration).

This stringent requirement was based upon the incident in Muhammad's life involving Aisha, who was accused of infidelity. Muhammad proclaimed her innocence, and at the same time instituted this legal requirement for sexual sins. Muhammad asked, "Why did they not produce four witnesses? Since they produce not witnesses, they verily are liars in the sight of Allah" (Sura 24:13).

Because of this legal requirement, it is nearly impossible to prove rape in Muslim countries governed by sharia law. Essentially, men can commit rape with impunity. Unless a woman can produce four credible male witnesses, the perpetrator goes free.

But the injustice doesn't end there. Often the rape victim's charge is used in court as an admission of adultery. So while the rapists go free, many of the woman are incarcerated. It has been estimated that in Pakistan as many as 75 percent of the women in prison are there because they were victims of rape.[15]

This may change due to a new bill passed by the Pakistan National Assembly. Currently, four males "must witness a rape in order to prosecute the criminal in Pakistan." Otherwise the woman can be accused of adultery. This new bill allows "DNA testing and circumstantial evidence to replace witness testimony in court."[16]

ISLAM AND THE CRUSADES

THE CRUSADES WERE A SERIES of military campaigns initiated by the pope in an effort to reclaim the Holy Land from the Muslims. The Crusaders left jobs and family to take up arms and fight in the cause for Christendom. The word *crusade* is taken from the Latin word *crux,* or cross.

Although there are some who portray the Crusades as merely a form of Western imperialism, there is much more to the story. One historian refers to them as "a mere episode in a struggle that has lasted 1,400 years, and were one of the few occasions when Christians took the offensive to regain the 'occupied territories' of the Holy Land."[1]

There were nine crusades. Most were sanctioned by the pope, but not all. These continued into the sixteenth century. The Crusades had a political, economic, and social impact that is still being felt even to this day.

How did the Crusades start?

In the 100 years after the death of Muhammad, Islam spread rapidly through the Middle East and even into Europe. This rapid expansion included Muslims conquering territories that formerly had been under the control of Christians. For example, the cities of Antioch, Alexandria, and Carthage had been centers of Christian thought. They all fell to Muslim armies engaged in jihad.

Jerusalem fell in 638, and this began centuries of the persecution of Christians. Early in the eighth century, 60 Christian pilgrims from Amorium were crucified. During that same period, the Muslim governor of Caesarea rounded up a group of pilgrims from Iconium and had them executed as spies. By the end of that century, the Muslim caliph in Jerusalem required that all Christians and Jews have their hands stamped with a distinctive symbol. By the ninth century, large numbers of Christians fled to Constantinople and other Christian cities.

A key date in the history of the Crusades is 1095. In that year, the Byzantine emperor Alexius I requested help from Pope Urban II. The Turks had already conquered much of the Byzantine Empire, and Alexius needed mercenaries to help him resist further Muslim advances. In fact, the city of Constantinople (perhaps the greatest Christian city in the world at that time) was being threatened. Pope Urban II, at the Council of Clermont, called upon Christians in Europe to respond to this plea.

While the pope knew that there was a need for the Christians to fight the Turks, he also knew that calling for people to help save Eastern Christendom alone would not motivate many. So in order to motivate the faithful, he set forth a second goal: to free Jerusalem and the birthplace of Christ from Muslim rule.

This was not some meager incentive; it was based on the fact that, in the years leading up to 1095, the Fatimid caliph, Abu 'Ali al-Hakim, had destroyed 30,000 churches, including the Church of the Holy Sepulchre in Jerusalem. Many Christians during that time considered al-Hakim to be the Antichrist.

The pope added another incentive to the call for military help: the possibility of the remission of sins. The Crusaders vowed to reach the Church of the Holy Sepulchre in Jerusalem in return for the pope's pardon for sins they had committed.

Pope Urban II probably reasoned that a crusade would serve to reunite Christendom and perhaps even bring the East under his control. But once the pope launched the first crusade, he had virtually no control over it. Those involved in the effort made their decisions about tactics and strategy apart from the pope. One writer points out that the army was held together by "feudal obligations, family ties, friendship, or fear."[2]

It is also important to understand that this was not seen as a holy war, at least not in the way Islam taught jihad as a holy war. It is true that in the fifth century, the Christian thinker Augustine had set for the foundations of what constituted a *just war.* But this idea did not include the concept of military engagement for the purpose of religious conversion. Leaders of nations might engage in warfare for a just cause, but war was not to be a tool of the church.[3] Unfortunately, the popes and Crusaders used Augustine's *just war* language and saw themselves as warriors for Christ.

What happened during the Crusades?

Although there were many military campaigns in those days that were called crusades, when we refer to the Crusades, we are talking about the nine military campaigns that took place between 1095 and 1272. These were launched from Western Europe against the Muslims in the Middle East.

1. *The First Crusade (1095–1099)*—this began when the Byzantine emporer Alexius I asked for Pope Urban II to send mercenaries to join a war against the invading Turks. It was the most successful of the nine crusades. The Crusaders defeated the Turks and were able to take control of Jerusalem. They established several states, including the Kingdom of Jerusalem.

2. *The Second Crusade (1145–1149)*—this was an unsuccessful

attempt to recapture a Crusader state (Edessa). It endangered the other Crusader states because of an unwise attack on Damascus.

3. *The Third Crusade (1189–1192)*—this was also known as the King's Crusade and was called by Pope Gregory in the wake of Saladin's capture of Jerusalem in 1187. Many famous people participated in this crusade, including King Richard the Lionheart of England and King Phillip of France.

4. *The Fourth Crusade (1201–1204)*—this was initiated by Pope Innocent but was diverted to Constantinople by someone seeking the Byzantine throne. After much confusion and misunderstanding, the Crusaders sacked the city in 1204. This shocked the Christian world and further weakened the Byzantine Empire.

5. *The Fifth Crusade (1217–1221)*—this crusade focused on Egypt with the assumption that by breaking Egyptian power, the Crusaders could recapture Jerusalem. While they did capture Damietta, they foolishly attacked Cairo and failed.

6. *The Sixth Crusade (1228–1229)*—a continuation of the Fifth Crusade. It came about because Emperor Frederick II had repeatedly vowed a crusade, but never kept his word. The pope excommunicated him in 1228. Frederick set sail to the Holy Land and was able to negotiate a truce that allowed Christians to live in Jerusalem. But because the city was defenseless, the Muslims were able to take the city in 1244. Christians were killed and many churches burned, including the Church of the Holy Sepulchre.

7. *The Seventh Crusade (1248–1254)*—the best-equipped crusade, led by Louis IX of France against Egypt from 1248 to 1254. In the midst of one battle, he was captured and later ransomed and returned to Europe.

8. *The Eighth Crusade (1270)*—this was also organized by Louis IX, who came to the aid of the Crusader states in Syria. The crusade was diverted to Tunis, where Louis died.

9. *The Ninth Crusade (1271–1272)*—this was organized by the

future Edward I of England, who had accompanied Louis IX on the Eighth Crusade. Little was accomplished, and Edward retired the following year after a truce.

What atrocities were committed during the Crusades?

Anyone who wants to criticize Christianity will most likely bring up the Crusades and talk about the atrocities committed by the Crusaders. It is certainly true that the Crusaders slaughtered Jews and Muslims in the sacking of Jerusalem. It is also true that the Crusaders even fought among themselves.

However, both Muslims and Christians committed atrocities and brought about considerable carnage. Also, during the Crusades, Muslims were merciless and barbaric in their treatment of Christians and Jews. Consider what the Turks did with the German and French prisoners captured in the First Crusade (prior to the sacking of Jerusalem). If the prisoners renounced Christ and converted to Islam, they were sent to the East. If they did not, they were slaughtered.

The Muslim leader Saladin was not as merciful as movies have portrayed him to be. For example, after defeating a large Latin army in 1187, he ordered the mass execution of all the Hospitallers and Templars left alive. He personally beheaded the nobleman Reynald of Chatillon. This is how Saladin's secretary described the scene:

> He ordered that they should be beheaded, choosing to have them dead rather than in prison. With him was a whole band of scholars and Sufis...[and] each begged to be allowed to kill one of them, and drew his sword and rolled back his sleeve. Saladin, his face joyful, was sitting on his dais; the unbelievers showed black despair.[4]

Saladin is best known for reconquering Jerusalem, and much is made of his willingness to allow his Christian opponents in

Jerusalem to live. But the true story is that he had originally planned to massacre all the Christians in the city after taking it back from the Crusaders. However, when the commander of Jerusalem threatened to destroy the city and kill all the Muslims inside the walls, Saladin changed his plan. He allowed the Christians to buy their freedom. If they could not do so, they were sold into slavery.[5]

How accurate are Hollywood films about the Crusades?

There have been a number of films made about the Crusades, with the most expensive film (over $150 million) being *Kingdom of Heaven*. It featured an all-star cast (Orlando Bloom, Jeremy Irons, Liam Neeson) and a massive publicity budget. So how accurate is it?

The script was full of politically correct clichés and does a disservice to those trying to understand this period of history. The film also invented a tolerance group known as the Brotherhood of Muslims, Jews, and Christians. No such group existed. It also makes it seem as if this brotherhood of tolerance would have held together if certain Christian extremists hadn't caused problems.

Jonathan Riley-Smith, a professor at Cambridge University and the author of *A Short History of the Crusades*, called the film "rubbish" and said it was "not historically accurate at all." He complained that it "depicts the Muslims as sophisticated and civilized, and the Crusaders are all brutes and barbarians. It has nothing to do with reality."[6]

Professor Jonathan Phillips, a lecturer at London University and the author of *The Fourth Crusade and the Sack of Constantinople*, said the film relied on an outdated portrayal of the Crusades and the Knights Templar. He says it is bad history: "The Templars as 'baddies' is only sustainable from the Muslim perspective, and 'baddies' is the wrong way to show it anyway. They are the biggest threat to the Muslims and many end up being killed because of their sworn vocation to defend the Holy Land."[7]

Did the Crusades accomplish anything?

Most would agree with the proposition that the Crusades are a dark chapter in Christian history. But did they accomplish anything of significance?

Some have argued that the movement of large European armies into Muslim territories stopped, at least for a while, the advance of Islam westward. If Godfrey of Bouillon and Richard the Lionheart had not fought in the Crusades, it is likely that the Muslim armies would have swept across Europe. Also, the presence of a Latin kingdom in Jerusalem provided a buffer zone between the Byzantine Empire and the Muslim world. It also forced Muslim leaders to focus their attention on defense instead of offense.

Others point to the rise of chivalry and knighthood due to the real and legendary acts of many of the European leaders during the Crusades. Crusading kings such as Richard the Lionheart and Louis IX were admired even by Muslims as men of valor and integrity. European rulers looked to the Crusader kings as models of how to integrate knighthood and Christianity.

The crusading spirit may have also been instrumental in encouraging many Europeans to sail to and explore the New World. For example, the voyage of Columbus coincides with the Reconquista that removed Muslim rule from Spain.

ISLAM AND THE CLASH OF CIVILIZATIONS

THE WESTERN WORLD FACES a major challenge from radical Islam in the twenty-first century.

One of the key issues is whether Islam is willing to adapt to the modern era. Islam is a seventh-century religion. Think about that statement for a moment—after all, most people would not consider Christianity a first-century religion. While Christianity began in the first century, the timeless message of the Bible is very relevant to our contemporary world.

In many ways, Islam is still stuck in the century in which it began. Will it ever adapt to the modern world?

Why do we face a clash of civilizations?

In the summer of 1993, Samuel Huntington published an article entitled "The Clash of Civilizations?" in the journal *Foreign Affairs*.[1] The article generated more controversy than any other article that appeared in the journal since the 1940s. And Huntington says it stirred up more debate than anything else he wrote in 1993.

Three years later, Samuel Huntington published a book titled *The Clash of Civilizations and the Remaking of World Order.* It became a bestseller and stirred more controversy. It seems worthy to revisit his comments and predictions, because they have turned out remarkably accurate.

Huntington's thesis is fairly simple: World history will be marked by conflicts between three principal groups—Western universalism, Muslim militancy, and Chinese assertion. Huntington says that in the post-Cold War world, "global politics has become multipolar and multicivilizational."[2] During most of human history, major civilizations were separated from one another and contact was intermittent or nonexistent. That pattern changed in the modern era (around A.D. 1500). For over 400 years, the nation states of the West (Britain, France, Spain, Austria, Prussia, Germany, and the United States) constituted a multipolar international system that interacted, competed, and fought wars against each other. During that same period of time, these nations also conquered and colonized nearly all other civilizations.

"Most people reading this have strong stomachs, so let me lay it out as baldly as I can: Much of what we loosely call the Western world will not survive this century, and much of it will effectively disappear within our lifetimes, including many if not most Western European countries. There'll probably still be a geographical area on the map marked as Italy or the Netherlands—*probably*—just as in Istanbul there's still a building called St. Sophia's Cathedral. But it's not a cathedral; it's merely a designation for a piece of real estate. Likewise, Italy and the Netherlands will merely be designations for real estate. The challenge for those who reckon Western civilization is on balance better than the alternatives is to figure out a way to save at least some parts of the West."[3]

—**Mark Steyn** in *Opinion Journal*

During the Cold War, global politics became bipolar. Western democracies led by the United States engaged in ideological, political, economic, and even military competition with communist countries led by the Soviet Union. Much of this conflict occurred in the Third World outside these two camps and was composed mostly of nonaligned nations.

Huntington argues that in the post-Cold War world, the principal actors are still the nation states, but they are influenced by more than just power and wealth. Other factors such as cultural preferences, commonalities, and differences are also influential. The most important groupings are not the three blocs of the Cold War era, but rather the major world civilizations. Most significant in our discussion here is the conflict between the Western world and Muslim militancy.

Bernard Lewis sees this conflict as a phase that Islam is currently experiencing—a phase in which many Muslim leaders are attempting to resist the modern world's influences (and in particular the Western world's influences) on their communities and countries. This is what he had to say about Islam and the modern world:

> Islam has brought comfort and peace of mind to countless millions of men and women. It has given dignity and meaning to drab and impoverished lives. It has taught people of different races to live in brotherhood and people of different creeds to live side by side in reasonable tolerance. It inspired a great civilization in which others besides Muslims lived creative and useful lives and which, by its achievement, enriched the whole world. But Islam, like other religions, has also known periods when it inspired in some of its followers a mood of hatred and violence. It is our misfortune that part, though by no means all or even most, of the Muslim world is now going through

such a period, and that much, though again not all, of that hatred is directed against us.[4]

This does not mean that all Muslims want to engage in jihad warfare against America and the West. But it does mean that there is a growing clash of civilizations. Muslims see the world divided into two camps, and this view intensifies the clash between the West and Islam. Bernard Lewis explains:

> In the classical Islamic view, to which many Muslims are beginning to return, the world and all mankind are divided into two: the House of Islam, where the Muslim law and faith prevail, and the rest, known as the House of Unbelief or the House of War, which it is the duty of Muslims ultimately to bring to Islam. It should by now be clear that we are facing a mood and a movement far transcending the level of issues and policies and the governments that pursue them. This is no less than a clash of civilizations—the perhaps irrational but surely historic reaction of an ancient rival against our Judeo-Christian heritage, our secular present, and the worldwide expansion of both. It is crucially important that we on our side should not be provoked into an equally historic but also equally irrational reaction against the rival.[5]

Does everyone believe we are in a clash of civilizations?

Not everyone accepts Samuel Huntington's analysis regarding conflict between Western democracies and Muslim militancy. For example, William Tucker believes that the actual conflict results from what he calls the Muslim intelligensia. He says

> that we are not facing a clash of civilizations so much as a conflict with an educated segment of a civilization that produces some very weird, sexually disoriented men.

> Poverty has nothing to do with it. It is stunning to meet the al Qaeda roster—one highly accomplished scholar after another with advanced degrees in chemistry, biology, medicine, engineering, a large percentage of them educated in the United States.[6]

Tucker's analysis is contrary to the many statements made to the effect that poverty breeds terrorism. While it is certainly true that many recruits for jihad come from impoverished situations, it is also true that many terrorist leaders are well-educated and highly accomplished.

William Tucker believes that those who wish to engage in jihad warfare against the West bear a striking resemblance to the student revolutionaries on American university campuses during the 1960s. He calls them "overprivileged children" whom he believes feel a need to prove themselves (and their manhood) in the world. He also believes that "this is confounded by a polygamous society where fathers are often distant from their sons and where men and women barely encounter each other as young adults."

Tucker says that our current conflict with Islam is not a war against a whole civilization. He points out that the jihad warriors are despised as much in their own countries as they are in the West.

"Many Muslims in Europe already consider themselves de facto autonomous, a community of believers opposed to the broader society of infidels. Jihadist networks now exist in every country west of the former Iron Curtain save Iceland...Most Muslims in Europe live in a parallel universe that has very little to do with the host country. Their mindset has nothing but contempt for the liberal concept of 'tolerance' and 'diversity,' and they possess a disdainful and hostile attitude to the host-society."[7]

—**Serge Trifkovic**, historian, journalist, and analyst

"The nature of the problem has always been spiritual. Like all totalitarian ideologies, Islam has an inherent tendency to the closing of the mind. The spirit of critical inquiry essential to the growth of knowledge is completely alien to it. Western engineers, military officers, and doctors could train their Muslim students, but the latter never managed to give more than what was imparted to them…There are symphony orchestras in Singapore, Seoul, and Beijing, but none in Amman, Ramallah, or Beirut."[8]

—**Serge Trifkovic**, historian, journalist, and analyst

"Egyptians are sick to death of the Muslim Brotherhood and its casual slaughter. The war between Fundamentalists and secular authorities in Algeria cost 100,000 lives."[9]

Tucker therefore concludes that we are effectively at war with a Muslim intelligentsia. These are essentially

> the same people who brought us the horrors of the French Revolution and 20th century Communism. With their obsession for moral purity and their rational hatred that goes beyond all irrationality, these warrior-intellectuals are wreaking the same havoc in the Middle East as they did in Jacobin France and Mao Tse-tung's China.[10]

One of the most-watched Internet video debates on Islam involved Wafa Sultan, who debated Al-Jazeera host Faisal al-Qasim and Islamic scholar Ibrahim Al-Khouli about Samuel Huntington's idea of a "clash of civilizations." The exchange took place on the 90-minute program "The Opposite Direction," with Sultan speaking via satellite from Los Angeles.[11] Here are two excerpts of what she said:

> The clash we are witnessing around the world is not a clash of religions, or a clash of civilizations. It is a clash between

two opposites, between two eras. It is a clash between a mentality that belongs to the Middle Ages and another mentality that belongs to the twenty-first century. It is a clash between civilization and backwardness, between the civilized and the primitive, between barbarity and rationality. It is a clash between freedom and oppression, between democracy and dictatorship. It is a clash between human rights, on the one hand, and the violation of these rights, on other hand. It is a clash between those who treat women like beasts, and those who treat them like human beings. What we see today is not a clash of civilizations. Civilizations do not clash, but compete.

The Muslims are the ones who began using this expression. The Muslims are the ones who began the clash of civilizations. The Prophet of Islam said, "I was ordered to fight the people until they believe in Allah and His Messenger." When the Muslims divided the people into Muslims and non-Muslims, and called to fight the others until they believe in what they themselves believe, they started this clash, and began this war. In order to stop this war, they must re-examine their Islamic books and curricula, which are full of calls for takfir and fighting the infidels.

What is the extent of the threat from radical Islam?

It is hard to estimate the extent of the threat from radical Islam, but there are some commentators who have tried to provide a reasonable estimate. Dennis Prager, for example, provides this overview:

> Anyone else sees the contemporary reality—the genocidal Islamic regime in Sudan; the widespread Muslim theological and emotional support for the killing of a Muslim who converts to another religion; the absence of freedom

in Muslim-majority countries; the widespread support for Palestinians who randomly murder Israelis; the primitive state in which women are kept in many Muslim countries; the celebration of death; the honor killings of daughters, and so much else that is terrible in significant parts of the Muslim world—knows that civilized humanity has a new evil to fight.[12]

Prager argues that just as previous generations had to fight the Nazis and the Communists, so this generation has to confront militant Islam. But he also notes something is dramatically different about this new threat. He says:

> Far fewer people believed in Nazism or in communism than believe in Islam generally or in authoritarian Islam specifically. There are one billion Muslims in the world. If just 10 percent believe in the Islam of Hamas, the Taliban, the Sudanese regime, Saudi Arabia, Wahhabism, bin Laden, Islamic Jihad, the Finley Park Mosque in London or Hizbollah—and it is inconceivable that only one of 10 Muslims supports any of these groups' ideologies—that means a true believing enemy of at least 100 million people.[13]

This very large number of people who wish to destroy civilization poses a threat that is unprecedented. Never has the world had to confront such large numbers of an enemy bent on destruction.

So what is the threat in the United States? Columnist Douglas MacKinnon has some chilling statistics. While he recognizes that most Muslims in the United States are peace-loving, still, the percentages he presents are sobering. He says:

> [I]f we accept the estimate that there are 6 million Muslim-Americans in our country, and 99% of them are law abiding citizens who are loyal to our nation, then that

means that there may be—may be—1% who might put a twisted version of Islamic extremism before the wellbeing of their fellow Americans. When you stop to think that 1% of 6 million is 60,000 individuals, that then seems like a very intimidating one percent. Let's go to the good side of extreme and say that 99.9 percent of all Muslim-Americans would never turn on their own government. That would still leave a questionable 1/10th of one per-cent—or 6,000 potential terrorist sympathizers.[14]

"What would a Socrates, Galileo, Descartes, or Locke believe of the present decay in Europe—that all their bold and cou-rageous thinking, won at such a great cost, would have devolved into such cheap surrender to fanaticism?

"Just think: Put on an opera in today's Germany, and have it shut down, not by Nazis, Communists, or kings, but by the simple fear of Islamic fanatics.

"Write a novel deemed critical of the Prophet Mohammed, as did Salman Rushdie, and face years of ostracism and death threats—in the heart of Europe no less.

"Compose a film, as did Theo Van Gogh, and find your throat cut in 'liberal' Holland.

"Or better yet, sketch a cartoon in postmodern Denmark, and then go into hiding.

"Quote an ancient treatise, as did the pope, and learn your entire Church may come under assault, and the magnificent stones of the Vatican offer no refuge."[15]

—**Victor Davis Hanson,** military historian and columnist

What implications does this clash of civilizations have for Christians?

This clash of civilizations has had a profound impact on missions. In the past, countries that were closed to the gospel tended to be

Communist. Even so, there was still a significant amount of Christian growth in the nations behind the Iron Curtain and Bamboo Curtain. Since the collapse of the Soviet Union, many of these countries have become more open to the gospel than ever before. Meanwhile, the persecution of Christians still persists in China.

But a new phenomenon has emerged. Muslim countries are now the most resistant to the message of Christianity. Mission work is limited or even nonexistent in many of these countries. This, I believe, represents the greatest challenge for missions in the twenty-first century: reaching the Muslim world for Christ. There are more than one billion Muslims in the world, making Islam the second largest religion in the world. And it is one of the fastest growing religions as well.

A second implication is related to the first. When Muslims see the West with its immorality and decadence, they reject it and Christianity. After all, they reason, the Western nations are Christian countries, and this is what they produce.

It is crucial for Christians to inform Muslims of the distinction between Christianity and Western society. Thus it is often helpful to agree with Muslims about many of their criticisms of Western culture. Doing this is disarming and provides you with an opportunity to explain that many Western countries (especially in Europe) are anything but Christian. From there you can focus the discussion on the Bible and Jesus Christ as a contrast to the Qur'an and Muhammad.

Whether we are missionaries overseas or in our backyard, we need to begin to understand the nature of Islam so we can be more effective at bringing the message of the gospel to the Muslims we meet. That's why we should stay informed of Muslim beliefs and culture.

ISLAM AND TERRORISM

WE LIVE IN A WORLD under constant threat of terrorist attacks. Rarely does a day go by without a reminder that we are not safe from terrorists and their actions against us.

Terrorism can be defined as the use of fear and violence against innocent citizens in an attempt to influence public opinion and policy. Terrorists usually do harm to noncombatants in an effort to create societal fear.

Terrorism has been called the "new warfare." But terrorists turn the notion of war on its head. Innocent noncombatants are the targets—terrorist warfare holds innocent people hostage and instills widespread fear into people.

Why have terrorists been so successful?

Terrorism has been practiced in the past, but not in the same way or to the same extent as today. Originally terror was used by governments against certain people within a given society. For example, the Reign of Terror in eighteenth-century France led to the execution of 25,000 people. Also, Marxist leaders used terror against their own citizens in order to bring about desired political and economic changes within their countries. But today, nearly all terrorist actions come from radical groups within Islam.

Terrorism against democratic governments has often been successful because these governments are accustomed to dealing with others within a legal structure. It's difficult, however, to deal with terrorists because they routinely operate outside of the law. Yet deterrence is just as much a part of justice as proper enforcement of the laws.

"Militant Islam wants to kill us just because we're alive and don't believe as they do. They've been killing us for decades. So it's time to stop pretending these terrorist incidents are mere episodic events and face the reality that our way of life is in grave danger. This threat is not just going to go away because we choose to ignore it. Some say we should try diplomacy. Yeah, well, tell me, how do we negotiate with people whose starting point is our death? Ask them to wait for ten years before they kill us? When good negotiates with evil, evil will always win and peace follows victory, not words issued by diplomats."[1]

—**Rush Limbaugh,** commentator

Democratic governments that fail to deter criminals inevitably spawn vigilantism—that is, a situation in which law-abiding citizens who have lost confidence in the criminal justice system take the law into their own hands. Two types of responses are emerging as a result of Western democracies failing to effectively defend themselves against terrorists. There are activists, who want to "bomb terrorists and terrorist nations back to the stone age." And there are pacifists, who want to retreat from the War on Terror and find ways to appease those who threaten Western society.

Terrorists have also been successful due to extensive media

exposure. Terrorists thrive on media attention, and news organizations (as well as Web sites and blogs on the Internet) have been all too willing to give terrorists the publicity they desire. When kidnappings, hijackings, and bombings are given prominent media coverage, governments start feeling pressure from their citizens to resolve the crisis. Often these governments end up capitulating to the demands of terrorists and their organizations. Encouraged by their initial success, terrorists usually try again. Appeasement, Churchill wisely noted, always whets the appetite, and recent successes by terrorists have made them hungry for more attacks.

Some news commentators have been unwilling to call terrorism for what it really is: wanton, criminal violence. Some news organizations refuse to even use the word *terrorist* in their broadcasts. Others argue that "one man's terrorist is another man's freedom fighter." But this simply is not true. Terrorists are not concerned about rights and human dignity. In fact, they end up destroying human rights in their alleged fight for such rights.

"We're in a war that I think is going to go on for a hundred years. Our institutional memory in the West is very short. We forget that from 632, when Muhammad wrote the Koran, until 1630-something, when the Ottoman Empire was defeated outside of Vienna, Islam—which is a militant belief system—was in a battle with Christianity. It subsided over recent years, but the Muslim nations, and particularly the radical Islamists, are no less aggressive today than they were through that thousand years when the West was in battle with them. What Osama bin Laden has done is simply to focus and give direction to the most radical elements in Islam—elements that believe that Allah can only be pleased when, by jihad, the infidels are destroyed, and that's us. It's everybody who isn't of their particular mind."[2]

—**Chuck Colson,** author and commentator

Are prisons becoming prime recruiting areas for terrorists?

A number of national security experts say that the radicalization and recruitment of terrorists in U.S. prisons presents a threat of "unknown magnitude." Prisons are fertile breeding grounds for radical thought. "Radical Islamists have been more active in European prisons, but there have been a handful of documented cases of Islamist radicalization in US prisons."[3]

Chuck Colson puts it this way: "I don't usually make predictions, but here's one I'll venture: If, God forbid, an attack by home-grown Islamist radicals occurs on American soil, many, if not most, of the perpetrators will have converted to Islam while in prison."[4]

A recent study by researchers from George Washington University and the University of Virginia, titled "Out of the Shadows," concluded that the United States is at risk of the same sort of homegrown terrorism that is currently plaguing other countries. These terrorists will come from prisons which "are a potential pool of recruits by terrorist groups…The sources of radicalization are incarcerated Islamic extremists and outside organizations that support them." Much of this material is provided by known al-Qaeda affiliates who urge Muslim prisoners "to wage war against non-Muslims who have not submitted to Islamic rule."[5]

How should we deal with terrorism?

We should begin by asking the question, What is a terrorist? Is a terrorist a common criminal? If terrorists are only common criminals, then they should merely be dealt with by their host governments. However, if terrorists are a foreign enemy of the government, then they should be treated as enemy combatants.

The answer to this question is no small issue. In recent decades, governments have oscillated in their answers to this question. How you answer will determine whether you bring terrorists to justice (treat them as criminals) or bring justice to terrorists (treat them as combatants). The Bible provides some guidance in Romans 13:

> Whoever resists authority has opposed the ordinance of God; and they who have opposed will receive condemnation upon themselves. For rulers are not a cause of fear for good behavior, but for evil. Do you want to have no fear of authority? Do what is good and you will have praise from the same; for it is a minister of God to you for good. But if you do what is evil, be afraid; for it does not bear the sword for nothing; for it is a minister of God, an avenger who brings wrath upon the one who practices evil (verses 2-4).

This passage of Scripture helps us make an important distinction in our analysis of terrorism. It shows that criminals are those who do evil and threaten civil peace. Any outside threat to the existence of the state is not a criminal threat but an act of war, which is also to be dealt with by the government.

In other words, criminals threaten the state from within. Foreign armies threaten the state from outside. In the case of seeking domestic peace, Romans 13 says governments should bring fear to those who are wrongdoers.

Evildoers should live in fear of government authorities, but that's not always the case with terrorists. Some terrorists live outside the laws of their host government and try to hide their covert activities, while others openly engage in terrorist training and actions with the approval of their host government.

Governments that give sanctuary and even approval to terrorists have often adopted the attitude that terrorists do them no harm, so why should they move against them and their organizations? In fact, their groups are not seen as a threat because they are acting out the host government's policies.

"Even in the past it was clear that terrorists claiming to act in the name of Islam had no compunction in slaughtering large numbers of fellow Muslims. A notable example was the blowing up of the American embassies in East Africa in 1998, killing a few American diplomats and a much larger number of uninvolved local passersby, many of them Muslims. There were numerous other Muslim victims in the various terrorist attacks of the last 15 years.

"The phrase 'Allah will know his own' is usually used to explain such apparently callous unconcern; it means that while infidel, i.e., non-Muslim, victims will go to a well-deserved punishment in hell, Muslims will be sent straight to heaven. According to this view, the bombers are in fact doing their Muslim victims a favor by giving them a quick pass to heaven and its delights—the rewards without the struggles of mar-tyrdom. School textbooks tell young Iranians to be ready for a final global struggle against an evil enemy, named as the U.S., and to prepare themselves for the privileges of martyrdom."[6]

—**Bernard Lewis,** professor and leading authority on Islam

By definition, terrorist groups and their host nations are enemies of the government when they capture and kill innocent civilians for military and foreign policy purposes. When terrorists attack, the government should not view them as criminals but as foreign soldiers who attempt to threaten the very existence of that government.

The tactics governments use to fight terrorism have to change. In the same way that it took traditional armies some time to learn how to combat guerilla warfare, so it is taking time for Western governments to realize that the rules for warfare must also be revised in response to terrorism.

Should we formally declare war on terrorism?

If Western governments say they are fighting a war on terrorism, shouldn't they formally declare war? This is a good question. Many have indeed called for a formal declaration of war rather than a more limited authorization for the use of power. A declaration of war would be an opportunity to thoroughly debate the issue as well as clearly define the identity of the enemy in this struggle.

The U.S. Constitution grants the following powers to Congress: "To define and punish piracies and felonies committed on the high seas, and offenses against the law of nations; to declare war, grant letters of marque and reprisal, and make rules concerning captures on land and water." Terrorist acts fall into at least two of the congressional provisions for dealing with attacks on the nation: They are (1) to punish offenses against the law of nations, and (2) to declare war.

In either case, there are strong constitutional grounds for taking action against terrorists. The difficulty comes in clearly identifying the enemy and being willing to risk offending many nations in the Middle East whom we consider allies. Congress should identify the enemy and thus define that group as a military target. Once Congress does this, many other issues are able to be resolved.

Military strategy should be deployed to hunt down the small groups of well-armed and well-funded men who hide within the territory of a host country. Political strategies should be developed that will allow the United States to work within a host country. The government must make it clear that it takes terrorist threats seriously.

Diplomacy also can play a part. Using diplomatic channels, we should make two things very clear to the host countries. First, they should catch and punish the members of terrorist groups as civilian criminals. Or second, they should extradite the enemy soldiers and give them up to an international court for trial.

If the host country fails to act on these two requests, we should make it clear that we see that country as being in complicity with the terrorist groups. When a government fails to exercise its civil responsibility, it leaves itself open to the consequences of allowing hostile military forces to exist within its borders.

"Without warfare and violence, we would have no country. America was born on the battlefield. (George III would never have let us go without a fight.)

"The Declaration of Independence was noble words penned on paper. It was the sword that gave them a reality. In this instance, the perpetrators of revolutionary violence included John Adams, Alexander Hamilton, Thomas Jefferson, Benjamin Franklin and George Washington—men of learning and ability all.

"Without warfare and violence the 11 states of the Confederacy would have successfully seceded in 1861, leaving us with two truncated nations. And the slaves would have been pickin' cotton for 'ole massah for at least a few decades more.

"Without warfare and violence in 1939–1945, today, half the world would be singing 'Deutschland uber Alles,' while the other half bowed to the honorable emperor of Japan.

"And without warfare and violence during the Cold War, the world would have been swallowed up by a monstrous ideology responsible for 100 million deaths in the 20th century."[7]

—**Don Feder,** former *Boston Herald* writer

Can the War on Terror be considered a just war?

The Christian response to war has ranged from pacifism to activism. But most Christians hold to what has come to be known as the "just war tradition." This view developed over some centuries and drew from Greek and Roman sources until it was formalized into a structure by Augustine.

There are seven elements to a just war. The first five apply to a nation "on the way to war" (*just ad bellum*) while the final two apply "in the midst of war" (*just in bello*):

1. Just cause. All aggression is condemned, only defensive war is legitimate.

2. Just intention. The only legitimate intention is to secure a just peace for all involved. Neither revenge nor conquest nor economic gain nor ideological supremacy are justified.

3. Last resort. War may be entered upon only when all negotiations and compromise have been tried and failed.

4. Formal declaration. Because the use of military force is the prerogative of governments and not of private individuals, a state of war must be officially declared by the highest authorities.

5. Limited objectives. If the purpose is peace, then unconditional surrender or the destruction of a nation's economic or political institutions is an unwarranted objective.

6. Proportionate means. The weaponry and the force used should be limited to what is needed to repel the aggression and deter future attacks (in order to secure a just peace).

7. Noncombatant immunity. Since war is an official act of government, only those who are officially agents of a government may fight, and individuals not actively contributing to the conflict should be immune from attack.

Although Christians may disagree over how to apply these principles in the current war on terrorism, these principles help provide a framework for the proper response to terrorists. For example, the principle of "proportionate means" leads to two conclusions:

- The military should not apply too severe a punishment. Calls for bombing cities of host countries in retaliation for terrorist actions should be rejected as inappropriate and unjust.

- The military should not apply too light a punishment. Host nations who harbor terrorists and refuse to punish or extradite terrorists should be pressured to do the right thing. Punishment could come in the form of economic embargoes, severing diplomatic relations, or even military actions. The punishment should be proportional to the terrorist act.

How does the "just war tradition" relate to terrorism?

Two types of objections often surface against the idea of a just war. First, there is the moral objection. Pacifists argue that it is never right to go to war and often cite certain biblical passages to bolster their argument. For example, Jesus said believers should turn the other cheek (Matthew 5:39). He also warned that "those who take up the sword shall perish by the sword" (Matthew 26:52).

But those statements must be understood in their contexts. In Matthew 5:39, Jesus is speaking to individual believers in His Sermon on the Mount, admonishing them not to engage in personal retaliation. In Matthew 26:52, Jesus tells Peter to put down his sword because the gospel should not be advanced by earthly weapons. But at the same time, we must remember that Jesus encouraged His disciples to buy a sword in order to protect themselves (Luke 22:36).

There is also the political objection. Critics say that the just war tradition applies only to nations and not to terrorists. Even so, that would not invalidate military action against Muslim countries that harbor terrorists.

What's more, the criticism is incorrect. Christian thought

about just war predates the concept of modern nation-states. So the principles regarding just war can apply to governments or terrorist organizations. Moreover, among the earliest uses of American military force in this country was against Barbary pirates, who were essentially the terrorists of the eighteenth century.

Is the profiling of terrorists ever justified?

Many social and political commentators have expressed concern about the possibility that the war on terrorism will involve racial or ethnic profiling. But this may be an inaccurate description of what takes place in the war on terrorism. For example, if you are robbed by a six-foot-tall black male wearing a red jacket, it is not racial profiling for law enforcement to look for such a person even if one element of the robber's characteristics is racial. What *would* be wrong is for law officers to pick up just any black male or just anyone wearing a red jacket.

So let's consider how a proper use of profiling might apply to the war on terrorism. If you have identified certain members of a terrorist cell, how would you be able to find the rest? You would look for common characteristics: age, ethnic background, religious background, and special training. If the members that have been identified are all male, young, Muslim, trained as pilots, and flying on one-way tickets, isn't it reasonable to expect that the other cell members are likely to fit that same profile?

Likewise, we have a profile for potential terrorist suspects. Most of the terrorist acts committed against the West have been carried out by Muslim men in their late teens to late thirties. This includes the following:

> Eleven Israeli athletes murdered at the Munich Olympics (1972); U.S. Marine barracks blown up in Beirut (1983); *Achille Lauro* cruise ship hijacked and an elderly,

disabled American passenger killed (1985); TWA Flight 847 hijacked (1985); Pan Am Flight 103 bombed (1988); World Trade Center bombed (1993); U.S. embassies bombed in Kenya and Tanzania (1998); USS *Cole* bombed (2000); Sept. 11, 2001; Madrid and London train bombings (2004 and 2005).[8]

Obviously profiling alone won't catch every terrorist. Critics point out that Timothy McVeigh (who blew up a federal office building in Oklahoma City) doesn't fit the aforementioned profile. One exception, however, doesn't invalidate the evidence that comes from three decades of violence instigated by radical Muslim terrorists. Profiling can, in fact, help government officials to better identify potential threats.

Is profiling legal? Some law scholars argue that profiling is constitutional if done in accordance with U.S. Supreme Court guidelines. This would mean that a person's ethnic background would not be the sole criteria for profiling. Other considerations might include age, gender, and behavior.

Fighting terrorism is going to be a long-term endeavor that will require clear thinking and wise actions. Terrorism has become the "new warfare," yet there are historical and biblical principles we can draw upon to better protect ourselves from this threat.

A FINAL WORD

THROUGHOUT THIS BOOK WE have focused on a number of topics related to Islam. My hope is that you've come to learn more about one of the fastest growing religions in the world.

I have also tried to provide a Christian response to Islam. The Bible admonishes us to defend our faith (1 Peter 3:15). We need to know how to respond to politically correct but inaccurate claims such as, Christians and Muslims worship the same God, and Islam is a religion of peace. Misconceptions about Islam are doing more harm than good to our society.

We have also looked at some of the serious concerns that can and should be raised about the lack of true human rights in Muslim countries and the threat of terrorism from those who believe they must fight in a jihad against infidels. These are sobering issues that must be addressed by our foreign policy.

Finally, we as Christians should seek opportunities to share our faith with our Muslim neighbors. First Timothy 2:3-4 says, "This is good and acceptable in the sight of God our Savior, who desires all men to be saved and to come to the knowledge of the truth." It is God's desire that all be saved. Thus, we must share the gospel with Muslims.

One of the most effective means of doing this is to show Muslims the Qur'an's exhortation to consult those who read the Scriptures that came before the Qur'an: "If you were in doubt as to what we have revealed unto you, then ask those who have been reading the Book from before; the Truth has indeed come to you from your Lord" (Sura 10:94). The Qur'an also says that to be a proper Muslim, one must read the "Before Books," which are the Old and New Testaments (Sura 4:136). These statements provide Christians with an open door to share the truths of the Bible with Muslims. Use these opportunities to share your faith with them.

If you would like more information on how to talk about Christianity to a Muslim, you may want to read some of the books I have listed in the bibliography. They will help you defend the faith, stand for truth, and witness to your Muslim neighbors.

BIBLIOGRAPHY

George Braswell, *Islam and America* (Nashville, TN: Broadman and Holman, 2005).

Emir Caner and Edward Pruitt, *The Costly Call* (Grand Rapids, MI: Kregel, 2005).

Ergun Caner and Emir Caner, *Christian Jihad* (Grand Rapids, MI: Kregel, 2004).

Ergun Caner and Emir Caner, *Unveiling Islam* (Grand Rapids, MI: Kregel, 2002).

Nonie Darwish, *Now They Call Me Infidel* (New York: Sentinel, 2006).

Timothy Demy and Gary Stewart, *In the Name of God: Understanding the Mindset of Terrorism* (Eugene, OR: Harvest House, 2002).

Brigitte Gabriel, *Because They Hate* (New York: St. Martin's Press, 2006).

Mark Gabriel, *Islam and Terrorism* (Lake Mary, FL: Frontline, 2002).

Norman Geisler, *Answering Islam: The Crescent in Light of the Cross* (Grand Rapids, MI: Baker, 2002).

Robert Morey, *The Islamic Invasion* (Eugene, OR: Harvest House, 1992).

Jerry Rassamni, *From Jihad to Jesus* (Chattanooga, TN: Living Ink Books, 2006).

Ron Rhodes, *The 10 Things You Need to Know About Islam* (Eugene, OR: Harvest House, 2007).

Robert Spencer, *The Politically Incorrect Guide to Islam (and the Crusades)* (Washington, DC: Regnery, 2005).

Robert Spencer, *The Truth About Muhammad* (Washington, DC: Regnery, 2006).

R.C. Sproul and Abdul Saleeb, *The Dark Side of Islam* (Wheaton, IL: Crossway, 2003).

Serge Trifkovic, *Defeating Jihad* (Boston: Regina Orthodox Press, 2006).

Serge Trifkovic, *The Sword and the Prophet* (Boston: Regina Orthodox Press, 2002).

NOTES

Chapter 1—The History of Islam

1. The history of Islam can be found in many places, including the biography by Ibn Ishaq, who collected the oral traditions of the eighth century. An English translation can be found in *The Life of Muhammad: A Translation of Ibn Ishaq's Sirat Rasul Allah,* Alfred Guillaume, trans. (Oxford: Oxford University Press, 1955).

2. Ibn Ishaq, *The Life of Muhammad: A Translation of Ishaq's Sirat Rasul Allah,* (New York: Oxford University Press, 1955), 106. Also al-Bukhari, vol. 6, book 65, no. 4953.

3. Bernard Lewis, "The roots of Muslim rage," *Atlantic Monthly,* September 1990, 47-60.

4. Ishaq, *The Life of Muhammad: A Translation of Ishaq's Sirat Rasul Allah*, 367-68.

5. Ibid., 515.

6. Ibid., 674-75.

7. Ibid., 675.

8. Ibid., 676.

9. Lewis, "The roots of Muslim rage."

Chapter 2—The Structure of Islam

1. Bernard Lewis, "Jihad vs. Crusade," *The Wall Street Journal,* September 27, 2001.

2. Interview from "Islam's assault on the West," *Renewing America's Mind* DVD (Dallas: Point of View, 2006).

3. Paul Johnson, "Relentlessly and thoroughly," *National Review,* October 15, 2001.

4. MSNBC's "Connected—Coast to Coast" program, July 7, 2006, http://counter terror.typepad.com/the_counterterrorism_blog/2005/07/interview_with_.html.

5. Chuck Colson, "Preparing for the Mahdi," *Breakpoint* commentary, August 14, 2006, http://www.breakpoint.org/listingarticle.asp?ID=1482.

6. Bernard Lewis, *The Crisis of Islam: Holy War and Unholy Terror* (New York: The Modern Library, 2003), 120-24.

7. Ibid., 128.

8. Ibid., 123-28.

9. Ibid., 129.

10. Robert Baer, *Sleeping with the Devil: How Washington Sold Our Soul for Saudi Crude* (New York: Crown Publishers, 2003), 89-90.

11. David Van Biema, "Wahhabism: Toxic faith?" *Time,* September 15, 2003, www. time.com/time/covers/1101030915/wwahhabism.html.

Chapter 3—The Theology of Islam

1. Al-Bukhari, vol. 6, book 61.

2. Annemarie Schimmel and Abdoldjavad Falaturi, *We Believe in One God* (New York: The Seabury Press, 1979), 31.

3. Ibid., 35.

4. Isma'il R. Al Faruqi, *Islam* (Nils, IL: Argus Communications, 1984), 9.

Chapter 4—A Christian Response to Islam

1. Abdullah Yusuf Ali, *The Holy Qur'an: Text, Translation, and Commentary* (Brentwood, MD: Amana Corporation, 1989), 49.

2. R.C. Sproul and Abdul Saleeb, *The Dark Side of Islam* (Wheaton, IL: Crossway Books, 2003), 33.

3. For more information, see Abdiyah Akbar Abdul-Haqq, *Sharing Your Faith with a Muslim* (Minneapolis, MN: Bethany Publishers, 1980), or Emir Fethi Caner and Ergun Mehmet Caner, *More Than a Prophet* (Grand Rapids, MI: Kregal Publications, 2003).

Chapter 5—Misconceptions About Islam

1. Interview from "Islam's Assault on the West," *Renewing America's Mind* DVD (Dallas: Point of View, 2006).

2. Daniel Allott, "Islam and violence," *The Washington Times,* December 4, 2006.

3. Chuck Colson, "The clash of civilizations: Revisiting the radical Islamic world-view," *Breakpoint* commentary, August 16, 2006, http://www.breakpoint.org/listingarticle.asp?ID=2187.

4. Bernard Lewis, *The Crisis of Islam: Holy War and Unholy Terror* (New York: The Modern Library, 2003), 76-79.

5. Ibid.

6. Ibid.

7. Ibid., 81.

8. Robert Spencer, "Khaybar, Khaybar; O Jews," *Human Events,* August 14, 2006, 660.

Chapter 6—Islam and Human Rights

1. Bernard Lewis, "Window on Islam," *Dallas Morning News,* July 9, 2006, 4P.

2. "Woman executed in Afghanistan," Associated Press News Service, March 30, 1997.

3. "Afghanistan execution for adultery," New York Times News Service, November 6, 1996.

4. Pact of Umar, http://en.wikipedia.org/wiki/Pact_of_Umar.

5. Umdat al-Salik (*Reliance of the Traveller*), 011.3-5.

6. Paul Marshall, *Their Blood Cries Out: The Worldwide Tragedy of Modern Christians Who Are Dying for Their Faith* (Dallas: Word, 1997) and Emir Fethi Caner and H. Edward Pruit, *The Costly Call: Modern-Day Stories of Muslims Who Found Jesus* (Grand Rapids, MI: Kregel, 2005).

7. Interview from "Islam's Assault on the West," *Renewing America's Mind* DVD (Dallas: Point of View, 2006).

8. Nawal El-Saadawi, quoted in *The Ideal Muslimah: The True Islamic Personality of the Muslim Woman as Defined in the Qur'an and Sunnah,* www.usc.edu/dept/MSA/humanrelations/womeninislam/idealmuslimah/.

9. Matthew Phillips, "Beliefwatch: School veil," *Newsweek,* November 13, 2006, 14.

10. "Umdat al-Salik, (manual of Islamic law), m 10.4.

11. Ibid., m 10.3.

12. Amnesty International, "Saudi Arabia: End secrecy end suffering: women," www.amnesty.org/ailib/intcam/saudi/briefing/4.html.

13. United Nations Children's Fund, "UNICEF: Child marriages must stop," March 7, 2001, www.unicef.org/newsline/01pr21.htm.

14. Lisa Beyer, "The women of Islam," *Time,* November 25, 2001.

15. Sisters in Islam, "Rape, zina, and incest," April 6, 2000, www.muslimtents.com/sistersinislam/resources/sdefini.htm.

16. "Numbers," *Time,* November 27, 2006, 24.

Chapter 7—Islam and the Crusades

1. Paul Johnson, "Relentlessly and thoroughly," *National Review Online,* October 15, 2001, http://www.nationalreview.com/15oct01/johnson101501.shtml.

2. Thomas F. Madden, *A Concise History of the Crusades* (Lanham, MD: Rowman & Littlefield Publishers, Inc., 1999), 10.

3. Ibid., 2.

4. Ibid., 78.

5. Ibid., 80.

6. Charlotte Edwardes, "Ridley Scott's new Crusades film panders to Osama bin Laden," *London Telegraph,* January 18, 2004, http://www.telegraph.co.uk/news/main.jhtml?xml=/news/2004/01/18/wcrus18.xml&sSheet=/news/2004/01/18/ixworld.html.

7. Ibid.

Chapter 8—Islam and the Clash of Civilizations

1. Samuel P. Huntington, "The clash of civilizations?" *Foreign Affairs,* Summer 1993, 22-49.

2. Samuel P. Huntington, *The Clash of Civilizations and the Remaking of World Order* (New York: Simon & Schuster, 1996), 21.

3. Mark Steyn, "It's the demography, stupid," *Opinion Journal,* January 4, 2006, http://www.opinionjournal.com/forms/printThis.html?id=110007760.

4. Bernard Lewis, "The roots of Muslim rage," *Atlantic Monthly,* September 1990, www.theatlantic.com/doc/prem/199009/muslim-rage.

5. Ibid.

6. William Tucker, "Overprivileged children," *American Spectator,* September 12, 2006, www.spectator.org/dsp_article.asp?art_id=10342.

7. Serge Trifkovic, "Europe's fellow travelers," *FrontPage Magazine,* August 18, 2006, http://www.frontpagemag.com/Articles/ReadArticle.asp?ID=23915.

8. Serge Trifkovic, "Decline without fall," *Chronicles of Culture,* August 2006, 38.

9. Tucker, "Overprivileged children."

10. Ibid.

11. The video clip from Al-Jazeera television that was seen on the Internet was produced by the Middle East Media Research Institute; http://switch5.castup .net/frames/20041020_MemriTV_Popup/video_480x360.asp?ai=214&ar=1050 wmv&ak=null.

12. Dennis Prager, "The Islamic threat is greater than German and Soviets threats were," May 19, 2006, www.townhall.com/columnists/DennisPrager/2006/03/28/ the_islamic_threat_is_greater_than_german_and_soviet_threats_were.

13. Ibid.

14. Douglas MacKinnon, "Home grown terrorists," August 25, 2006, www.townhall .com/columnists/DouglasMacKinnon/2006/08/25/home_grown_terrorists.

15. Victor Davis Hanson, "Traitors to the enlightenment," *National Review Online,* October 2, 2006, http://article.nationalreview.com?q=M2JlMzJhNjIxZGZkYjdm ZGU0ZGUyOWM3MzEwMTk0ZWQ=.

Chapter 9—Islam and Terrorism

1. Rush Limbaugh, commentary on *CBS Evening News,* September 7, 2006.

2. Interview with Chuck Colson, "Worldviews in conflict: Christianity & Islam," *Intercessors for America Newsletter,* September 2006.

3. Alexandra Marks, "Islamist radicals in prison: How many?" *Christian Science Monitor,* September 20, 2006, www.csmonitor.com.

4. Chuck Colson, "What's hidden in the shadows? Radical Islam and US prisons," September 26, 2006, www.townhall.com.

5. Ibid.

6. Bernard Lewis, "August 22: Does Iran have something in store?" *The Wall Street Journal,* August 8, 2006, http://www.opinionjournal.com/extra/?id=110008768.

7. Don Feder, "Fighting terror with estrogen," August 31, 2006, *FrontPage Magazine,* http://frontpagemag.com/Articles/ReadArticle.asp?ID=24168.

8. Kathleen Parker, "Do profile; don't tell," August 16, 2006, http://www.townhall .com/columnists/KathleenParker/2006/08/16/do_profile;_dont_tell.